ILLUSTRATED LIBRARY OF COOKING

VOLUME 13 Pot-Sal

Ever wondered how to cope
gracefully when friends pop
in unannounced? Or the best
way to cook a huge roast? Or
what to do about leftovers?
Volume 13 has most of the
answers. It includes: Potluck
Luxury . . . Roasts, Juicy and
Tender . . . Roasts on the
Comeback Trail . . . and in
addition, a huge portfolio of
salads and salad dressings.

ROCKVILLE HOUSE PUBLISHERS, INC.
ROCKVILLE CENTRE, NEW YORK 11570

Family Circle®

Illustrated Library of

COOKING

YOUR READY REFERENCE FOR A LIFETIME OF GOOD EATING

Picture Credits:

Family Circle • George Nordhausen

Copyright © 1972 The Family Circle, Inc.
All rights reserved under International and Pan-
American Copyright Conventions.
Printed in the United States of America

Salads need not come to the table in the proverbial salad bowl. Try serving a crisp slaw or salad in green or red pepper cups, a vegetable salad in squash boats or a fruit salad in a scooped-out avocado or serrated melon.

Table of Contents

POTLUCK LUXURY: SERVING SURPRISE GUESTS

"Potluck," says Webster, is "the regular meal available to a guest for whom no special preparations have been made." Which today means scaring up a meal out of whatever you have on hand.

The best way to cope is to have a well-armed cupboard, freezer and refrigerator. Particularly handy to have are mixes (for rolls, muffins, piecrusts, biscuits, cookies), also those deliciously versatile refrigerated crescent rolls that can double as top crusts, flaky pastries, even as the puff pastry blanket that wraps up a lavish Beef Wellington.

Good insurance, too, against drop-in guests is a hearty line-up of canned soups, which make superb last-minute sauces; canned tomatoes, tomato pastes and sauces, ever-so-essential for last-minute pizza and pasta; canned fruits (for salads, desserts, garnishes); ice creams and jiffy puddings; an assortment of chips and crackers and cookies, and, of course, some meat in both freezer and refrigerator. Always good bets: a ham steak, ground beef, maybe a frozen ready-to-bake meat loaf, and a collection of cold cuts—both meats and cheeses. Salad greens, it goes without saying, are indispensable and so are tomatoes, olives, pickles, relishes and bottled salad dressings.

With these foods on hand, you're set for almost anyone who may drop in—the husband's boss, the kids' teenage crew or friends who just happen by at mealtime.

Stack up sliced tomatoes, cheese, chicken, bacon and lettuce, serve on toast points for a club-style salad.

SERVING SURPRISE GUESTS

WHEN SOMEONE DROPS IN UNANNOUNCED AT LUNCHTIME, SERVE:

Hot Consommé
Tomato Clubs
Toast Points or Crisp Crackers
On-Hand Pudding or Ice Cream   Cookies
Coffee   Tea

Tomato Clubs
Build this triple-deck "sandwich-salad" of thick juicy tomato slices with lots of meat and cheese between.
Makes 4 servings

4 large tomatoes
1½ teaspoons sugar
1½ teaspoons salt
¼ teaspoon pepper
4 slices process Swiss cheese (from an 8-ounce package)
8 slices white bread
    Mayonnaise or salad dressing
    Leaf lettuce
8 slices cooked chicken, turkey or ham
8 slices crisp bacon
    Stuffed green and ripe olives
    Bottled blue-cheese salad dressing

1 Peel tomatoes and cut out stem ends; cut each into 3 thick slices, keeping slices in order.
2 Combine sugar, salt and pepper in a cup. Cut cheese slices into ¼-inch-wide strips.
3 Toast bread; trim crusts, then spread toast

1543

with mayonnaise or salad dressing. Halve 4 slices diagonally; place 1 whole slice and 2 halves on either side on each of 4 serving plates as a base for "sandwiches."

4 Build each this way: Place stem end slice of tomato, cut side up, on toast; sprinkle with seasoning mixture; top with lettuce, chicken, turkey or ham slices, tomato slice, more seasoning mixture, lettuce, cheese strips, bacon, remaining tomato slice and any remaining seasoning mixture.

5 Hold together with a long wooden pick threaded with green and ripe olives. Serve with blue-cheese dressing or with your favorite mayonnaise or salad dressing, if you wish.

WHEN TEENAGERS ARRIVE BY THE CARLOAD, SERVE:

ANY Pizza
(Five "Quickie" Choices Follow)
Vegetable Stick Nibbles
Milk   Soft Drinks

Ham-and-Salami Pizza

Such adaptability! Here two popular meats go with pineapple for a different topping.
Bake at 450° for 20 minutes. Makes 12 servings

1 package hot-roll mix
1 cup warm water
2 tablespoons vegetable oil
2 cans (8 ounces each) tomato sauce with cheese
8 slices round pizza cheese (from two 6-ounce packages)
12 slices boiled ham (from two 6-ounce packages)
6 slices pineapple (from a 1-pound, 14-ounce can), drained
12 slices salami (from two 6-ounce packages)

1 Prepare hot-roll mix with warm water, following label directions for pizza dough; divide in half. Roll each to an about-15-inch round on a lightly floured pastry cloth; fit into ungreased 14-inch pizza pans. Brush each with vegetable oil; spread with tomato sauce.

2 Cut 6 of the cheese slices in half and remaining 2 in quarters. Roll up ham slices; halve pineapple slices.

3 Arrange topping on each pizza this way: Place 6 half slices of cheese, rounded side out, in crust in a circle next to edge. Place 6 salami slices, slightly overlapping cheese, in a second ring; place 6 ham rolls, spoke fashion, between cheese slices. Lay 6 half slices pineapple over ham; place 4 cheese quarters in center.

4 Bake in very hot oven (450°) 20 minutes, or

1544

until sauce bubbles up and crust is golden. Cut in wedges.

Antipasto Pizza

Mushrooms, onions and green peppers put your homemade touch on a versatile packaged mix.
Bake at 450° for 20 minutes. Makes 6 servings

1 package pizza mix with sausage or pepperoni
3 slices Swiss cheese (from an 8-ounce package)
1 large onion, peeled and cut in 6 thin slices
1 small green pepper, seeded and cut in 6 rings
8 small fresh mushrooms, washed, trimmed and sliced
7 slices bacon

1 Prepare crust from package of pizza mix, following label directions; pat into a 12-inch pizza pan. Spread evenly with sauce and sprinkle with cheese from package.

2 Cut Swiss-cheese slices in half crosswise; place, spoke fashion, over sauce. Arrange onion slices in pepper rings around edge; place mushroom slices between peppers and in center.

3 Bake in very hot oven (450°) 20 minutes, or until sauce bubbles up and crust is golden.

4 While pizza bakes, sauté bacon until almost crisp in a medium-size frying pan, then before removing from pan, roll each slice around the tines of a fork to make a curl; hold each in place with a wooden pick, if needed. Drain on paper toweling. Place on onion rings and in center of pizza. Cut in wedges.

Wiener Winner Pizza

Add a simple bonus topping to frozen pizza, and no one will guess your speedy secret.
Bake at 450° for 12 minutes. Makes 4 servings

1 frozen large cheese pizza
2 frankfurters
1 can (about 1 pound) whole peeled tomatoes
Bottled Italian salad dressing
8 anchovy fillets (from a 2-ounce can), drained

1 Remove frozen pizza from package and place on a large cookie sheet.

2 Slice frankfurters in half lengthwise, then crosswise to make 8 pieces; arrange, spoke fashion, on top of pizza.

3 Drain tomatoes well, saving juice to add to stew or soup; cut each tomato in 8 wedges. Arrange around and between frankfurters; brush lightly with Italian dressing. Place anchovies over tomatoes.

The easiest way to cope with hungry teenagers—pizza! Keep roll mix handy, also pizza cheese, sauce, salami.

4 Bake in very hot oven (450°) 12 minutes, or until cheese is bubbly. Cut in wedges.

●

Mexicali Pizza
Peppery chili filling tops a crust of ready-to-go refrigerated rolls.
Bake at 425° for 20 minutes. Makes 8 servings

½ pound ground beef
1 can (1 pound) tomatoes
1 can (8 ounces) kidney beans, drained
1½ teaspoons chili powder
1 teaspoon sugar
½ teaspoon salt
¼ teaspoon pepper
2 packages refrigerated crescent dinner rolls
2 cups grated Cheddar cheese
16 large stuffed green olives, halved
4 cups shredded lettuce

1 Shape ground beef into a patty; brown in a large frying pan 5 minutes on each side; break into chunks.
2 Stir in tomatoes, kidney beans, chili powder, sugar, salt and pepper. Simmer, stirring several times, 15 minutes, or until slightly thickened.
3 Separate rolls into triangles, following label directions. Press evenly over bottom and up side of a 14-inch pizza pan. Spoon tomato sauce into crust; sprinkle with grated cheese. Arrange olive halves on top.
4 Bake in hot oven (425°) 20 minutes, or until sauce bubbles up and crust is golden. Cut in wedges; sprinkle with shredded lettuce.

●

Pizza Miniatures
With canned meat sauce, smoky sausage and English muffins, you can keep the supply coming piping-hot—and fast!
Bake at 400° for 10 minutes. Makes 8 servings

8 English muffins, split and toasted
2 tablespoons olive oil
1 can (about 11 ounces) spaghetti sauce with meat
1 teaspoon leaf oregano, crumbled
¼ teaspoon crushed red pepper
1 package (8 ounces) smoked sausage links, sliced thin
1 package (8 ounces) mozzarella cheese, grated

1 Brush muffin halves with olive oil. Place on a large cookie sheet.
2 Mix spaghetti sauce, oregano and red pepper in a small bowl; spoon about 1 tablespoonful over each muffin half. Arrange sausage slices in rings on top; sprinkle with cheese.

1546

3 Bake in hot oven (400°) 10 minutes, or until cheese is bubbly hot.

WHEN FRIENDS STOP BY LATE OF A WINTRY AFTERNOON, SERVE:

Cobble Buns
Rabbit Ham Rounds
Quick Viennese Mocha

Cobble Buns
Seasoned shrimps, sausages, mushrooms and chunks of zucchini broil on skewers, then slide into toasty rolls.
Makes 8 sandwiches

2 small zucchini, trimmed and sliced 1 inch thick
1 pound frozen, cooked, shelled and deveined shrimps, thawed
2 cans (4 ounces each) Vienna sausages, drained
8 small fresh mushrooms, washed and trimmed
½ cup bottled Italian salad dressing
8 split frankfurter rolls
Butter or margarine
8 pitted ripe olives
½ cup bottled chili sauce
2 tablespoons prepared mustard

1 Parboil zucchini in boiling salted water in a small saucepan 5 minutes, or until crisply tender; drain thoroughly.
2 Thread zucchini through rind with shrimps, sausages and mushrooms onto each of 8 skewers, dividing evenly; place in a single layer in a shallow dish.
3 Drizzle with Italian dressing; cover. Chill several hours to season.
4 Just before serving, toast frankfurter rolls in broiler; spread with butter or margarine; keep warm. Place kebabs in a single layer on rack in broiler pan.
5 Broil, 4 to 6 inches from heat, 5 minutes; turn. Broil 5 minutes longer, or until shrimps are tender.
6 Push foods off each skewer into a buttered roll; garnish each with a ripe olive.
7 Blend chili sauce and mustard in a cup. Serve separately to spoon over sandwiches.

●

Rabbit Ham Rounds
Creamy-smooth cheese sauce goes over meat and hard-cooked eggs piled on muffin halves.
Makes 8 sandwiches

2 tablespoons butter or margarine

Cobble Buns, Rabbit Ham Rounds and Quick Viennese Mocha take the edge off appetites on a cold day.

4 cups grated Cheddar cheese (1 pound)
2 teaspoons dry mustard
½ cup cream for whipping
1 teaspoon Worcestershire sauce
4 English muffins, split and toasted
16 thin slices boiled ham (from three 6-ounce packages)
4 hard-cooked eggs, shelled and sliced

1 Melt butter or margarine in the top of a double boiler over simmering, *not boiling,* water.
2 Mix grated cheese with mustard in a medium-size bowl; stir into butter or margarine slowly, stirring constantly and keeping over simmering water, until cheese melts and mixture is very smooth and thick. Stir in cream and Worcestershire sauce.
3 When ready to serve, place each muffin half on a serving plate; top with two folded slices of ham and four or five egg slices. Spoon hot cheese sauce over all. Serve hot.

Quick Viennese Mocha

With two instants on hand, just mix, pour and serve—it's that simple.
Makes 6 servings

¼ cup cream for whipping

1 tablespoon sugar
6 cups milk
4 tablespoons instant cocoa mix
2 tablespoons instant coffee powder
6 long cinnamon sticks

1 Beat cream with sugar until stiff in a small bowl.
2 Heat milk just to scalding in a large saucepan; stir in cocoa mix and coffee until dissolved.
3 Pour into large cups or mugs; top each with a spoonful of whipped cream. Add a cinnamon stick for a stirrer, or sprinkle cream with ground cinnamon, if you wish. Serve hot.

WHEN YOUR HUSBAND CALLS AT 4 P.M. AND SAYS HE'S BRINGING THE BOSS HOME TO DINNER, SERVE:

1547

Tropical Fruits
Apricot Ham Steak
Baked Potato Cups
Tossed Green Salad   Chive Dressing
Corn Muffins (from a mix)
Buttered Toasted Pound Cake (store-bought)
à la Mode
Coffee

Tropical Fruits
Makes 6 servings

1 medium-size avocado, peeled, seeded and sliced
1 papaya or mango or 2 peaches, pared, seeded and diced
¼ cup vegetable oil
3 tablespoons lemon juice
¼ teaspoon salt
⅛ teaspoon pepper
  Dash of ground ginger
1 small bunch seedless green grapes, washed and stemmed

1 Place avocado and papaya, mango or peaches in separate shallow dishes or pie plates.
2 Combine vegetable oil, lemon juice, salt, pepper and ginger in a small jar with tight-fitting cover; shake well to mix. Pour over avocado and papaya; toss lightly to coat. Cover; chill.
3 When ready to serve, drain dressings from fruits and save for salad for another meal. Spoon avocado slices into individual sherbet glasses, dividing evenly. Top with papaya and grapes.

Apricot Ham Steak
Be thrifty and buy a half ham, have a thick slice cut for this party-style dish, then save for another day.
Bake at 325° for 1 hour and 15 minutes. Makes 6 servings

1 slice cook-before-eating or fully cooked ham, cut 2 inches thick
  Whole cloves
¼ cup firmly packed brown sugar
1 can (1 pound) peeled whole apricots

1 Score fat on ham slice into diamonds; stud with whole cloves. Place in shallow baking pan; sprinkle with sugar.
2 Drain syrup from apricots into 1-cup measure; pour ⅓ cup of the syrup over ham. (Use any remaining syrup for sweetening fruit beverages.)
3 Bake in slow oven (325°), basting often with syrup in pan, 1 hour. Arrange drained apricots on top of ham. Bake, basting both ham and fruit, 15 minutes longer, or until richly glazed.
4 Lift onto heated serving platter; carve into ½-inch-thick slices.

Baked Potato Cups
How inviting these fluffy potatoes look and taste with their nippy green-onion topper!
Bake at 325° for 1½ hours. Makes 6 servings

6 baking potatoes, scrubbed and dried
4 tablespoons (½ stick) butter or margarine
1 teaspoon salt
⅛ teaspoon pepper
  Milk
2 green onions, chopped

1 Bake potatoes in slow oven (325°) 1½ hours, or until soft when pressed with fingers. (Low temperature is used so potatoes can bake in same oven with ham. If baking alone, bake in hot oven [400°] 1 hour.)
2 Cut each potato in half crosswise; scoop out

1548

Great beginning: a crystal goblet of Tropical Fruits.

Apricot Ham Steak, Baked Potato Cups with Chive Dressing make an easy, elegant meal for impromptu guests.

with a spoon into top of a small double boiler. (Save 6 perfect shells for Step 4; discard remaining.)

3 Stir butter or margarine, salt, and pepper into potatoes, then beat in milk a little at a time, until fluffy-light. (If potatoes must stand for a while before serving, cover top of double boiler and set over hot water.)

4 Heap hot potato mixture into shells, dividing evenly; sprinkle with onion.

Chive Dressing
Makes 1 cup

 1 cup mayonnaise or salad dressing
 ¼ cup finely chopped parsley
 1 tablespoon cider vinegar
 1 tablespoon chopped chives

Blend all ingredients together in a small bowl. Cover and chill until serving time.

ROASTS, JUICY AND

TENDER

ROASTS, JUICY AND TENDER:
BEEF, VEAL, LAMB, PORK AND HAM

What more elegant than a giant roast, cooked to perfection and set off by just the right combination of vegetables and salad?

Beef, of course, is America's great favorite. Has been since the hell-for-leather days of cowboys and ranchers around the turn of the century. To many of us, in fact, *ROAST* means *BEEF.*

It shouldn't, because other roasts are equally good. And many are more economical than beef because there is less demand for them. Veal can be exquisite, especially when braised in the company of vegetables in a savory gravy. Lamb is luscious, be it a tender young leg, a shoulder or breast stuffed and pot-roasted. Pork, too, is a winner—fresh pork loin or shoulder or fresh ham; and America's second favorite—ham, which is simply pork that has been cured and/or smoked.

A choice loin or rib roast needs nothing more than a gentle cooking in the oven without a cover, without anything added except, perhaps, a judicious rubbing of herbs. But the tougher cuts, those from well-exercised parts of the animal like shoulder, breast, round or rump, are better when pot-roasted or braised so that their sinewy tissues turn succulent and tender.

In the pages that follow, you'll find dozens of recipes for roasting and pot-roasting beef, veal, lamb, pork and ham, all of them from FAMILY CIRCLE'S file of favorite recipes.

 Juicy, pink Delmonico Beef Roast with Yorkshire Puffs.

BEEF, VEAL, LAMB, PORK AND HAM

(WORK)
HOW TO SAVE (MONEY) WITH ROASTS AND
(TIME)
POT ROASTS

Cook Big

Watch for advertised specials on large cuts of meat: Ribs of beef, a whole pork loin, boned and rolled veal roast, a whole ham. Not only is your choice a bargain in price per pound, but a big cut means meat for several meals. It takes very little longer to cook a larger-than-usual piece of meat, as the bigger the cut, the fewer minutes per pound. For example, a 5-pound rib of beef needs about 2 hours for roasting rare, whereas an 8-pound roast takes less than an hour longer. Besides having meat ready for 2 or 3 meals, just think of the time and work you save.

Cook Double

Buy two or even three kinds of meat that will roast in approximately the same time, and cook them together. For example, in 2½ hours you can bake a 7-pound cook-before-eating ham while roasting a 4-pound boned and rolled beef roast to rare. Or a 6-pound leg of lamb and a 5-to-6-pound smoked picnic take just 3 hours. They are then ready to turn into favorite dishes or slice into your own thrifty cold cuts.

ROASTS, JUICY AND TENDER

HOW MUCH TO BUY?

It's easy to count noses and buy enough frank-furters or chops to go around. But when buying roasts, a little arithmetic is needed. Good buying rules, worth knowing any time:

Boneless Meat—Allow ¼ pound for each serving. This includes rolled roasts, boneless roasts beef and pork tenderloin.

Small-Bone Meats—Allow ⅓ to ½ pound for each serving. These are bone-in roasts—rib, leg of lamb, pork loin, shoulder and chuck cuts.

Large-Bone Meats—Allow ¾ to 1 pound for each serving.

YOUR MEAT TIMETABLE

Choose the kind and weight of meat to match the time you plan to be around the house.

	1¾ to 2¾ hours	3 to 4 hours
	Pound weight	Pound weight
BEEF		
Rib Roast (rare)	4 to 6	8 to 9
Rolled Roast	4	6
Eye Roast	4	
★Pot Roast		3 to 5
★Corned Beef		3 to 4
★Fresh Brisket		3 to 4
★Tongue		3 to 4
PORK		
Shoulder Butt		4 to 5
Loin Roast		4 to 6
Ham (cook-before-eating)	5 to 7	9 to 12
Fresh Shoulder		5
★Smoked Picnic	5	8
LAMB		
Leg (whole)		6 to 8
Leg (half)	4	
Shoulder		4 to 6
Rolled Shoulder	3 to 4	5
VEAL		
Shoulder		5 to 6
Rump	3	5 to 6
Leg		6 to 8
Rolled Roast	4	6 to 8

Starred (★) meats can be simmered on top of the range

MEAT-STORAGE TIPS

Our supermarkets tempt us to dawdle, especially at the meat counter, where so many attractive cuts are displayed chilly-cold in refrigerated cases. But meat is perishable. Once it's bagged and put in the car, it should be rushed home. And from here on, it's up to us to handle it every bit as carefully as our supermarket has. These 5 pointers tell how:

1. Unwrap Fresh Meat—Leave meat bought at the self-service counter in its wrapper if you plan to use it that day. Otherwise, slit the covering so air can get to the meat. Unwrap completely any special-order, market-wrapped cut.

2. Chill Fast—Put meat in the coldest part of your refrigerator, or in the meat compartment, if it is to be used within 2 to 3 days. Leaving it uncovered, or loosely covered, allows cold air to circulate around it, drying the surface slightly. This is good, as it helps to keep the meat fresh.

3. Keep Cured Meats Wrapped—Store smoked meats—ham, bacon, cold cuts, frankfurters—in their original wrappers alongside fresh meat in the refrigerator. Curing helps to preserve quality, but for best flavor, plan to use within 2 weeks. Cured meats do not freeze well because of their saltiness. In an emergency, you can do it, but plan to keep them no longer than 2 months.

4. Look Ahead—Freeze Some—If you buy more meat than you can use in 2 to 3 days, unwrap it completely, rewrap in moistureproof paper or foil, and quick-freeze in the coldest part of your freezer.

5. Take Care with Cooked Meat—Whether it's meat left from a meal or cooked specially for another day, cool it quickly before wrapping. If you wish, halve a large roast, then put it, uncovered, in the refrigerator so cold air will circulate around it. When cold, wrap loosely or pack in a covered container and hustle back into the refrigerator. Reheat just what you need at one time, but plan to use all within a day

POT ROASTS: HOW TO GET YOUR MONEY'S WORTH

Mention pot roast, and most of us think beef. But dozens of cuts of veal, pork and lamb rate just as high in flavor, take to cooking this no-watch way and go easy on your budget. To stretch your meat money farthest, keep in mind these in-store and at-home pointers.

Step 1: Learn the Cuts

Almost every week, you'll find one or more pot-roasting cuts "on special" to tempt you to try something different or to stock up on an old favorite for your freezer. A few to consider:

Beef—Among the chunky 3- to 6-pound roasts, you'll find rump with bone in, boneless or rolled; sirloin tip, boneless and sometimes rolled and tied; heel of round, a triangular boneless piece; fresh boneless brisket; English, or Boston, roast, a rectangular cut that's thicker at one end and bone-in or boneless; blade- or arm-bone chuck, easily identified by a long narrow bone or a small round one; Swiss steak, a popular 1- to 2-inch-thick piece cut from the round.

Live-aloners or twosome families can take advantage of short ribs or round steak to get just the amount of meat they want without having lots left over.

Veal—This is young beef with very little fat, so pot-roasting is the best cooking method for rolled roasts from shoulder, leg, rump or breast; bone-in blade- or arm-shoulder roasts; brisket; breast; cutlets; steaks; and chops.

Lamb—These cuts are especially suitable for pot-roasting: Boned and rolled shoulder or breast; square-cut or cushion shoulder; sirloin; breast; shank; neck slices; shoulder steaks and chops.

Pork—Among the leading choices are Boston butt, sometimes rolled; fresh picnic shoulder with bone, or boned and rolled; fresh pork leg; whole tenderloin; spareribs; and thick rib or shoulder chops.

Step 2: Buy Wisely

As always, the law of supply and demand plays its part. Because oven roasts and broiling steaks and chops are the most popular and because there are only so many of these cuts on each animal, their cost is the highest. What remains shows up on the meat counter as the less-tender and, consequently, thriftier choices. Another point to remember is that within the pot-roast family itself, prices will vary, again depending on popularity. What does all this signify when you're shopping? Simply that you should stop, look and compare before you buy.

In today's supermarket more and more cuts are being sold boneless, because their ease and convenience in carving are a boon to homemakers. But, as you know, boning, trimming and rolling take time and labor, and these extra services raise the price. Even so, keep in mind that you are getting more servings per pound than with bone-in meat, and although the cost is higher at the store, it may not turn out this way at the dinner table. To illustrate the point, let's do a little arithmetic: Suppose that center-cut bone-in chuck sells for 69¢ a pound. According to the United States Department of Agriculture, you'll need ¾ pound per serving. This figures out to 52¢. Now look at the same cut sold boneless at $1.28 a pound. The Government recommends ⅓ pound per serving, or a cost, in this case, of 43¢. So, in the final analysis, the boneless cut starts at 59¢ more a pound but ends up at 9¢ less.

How much should you buy? Total the number of servings you need for one or more meals, then allow ⅓ pound per serving for boneless roasts and ½ to ¾ pound for bone-in kinds. Another reminder: Good buys do come in big packages. Cook enough meat at one time to have some left for a bonus meal, and you save three ways—in effort, minutes and money.

Step 3: Store Properly

When you get home from shopping, loosen the wrapper on prepackaged meat if you plan to keep it more than one day, then place the package in the coldest part of your refrigerator. Prepackaged meat can be frozen just as it comes from the store for one to two weeks. But for a longer period, overwrap or rewrap the package in heavy foil to prevent the meat from drying.

Step 4: Cook Correctly

In general, follow these simple rules, whatever your choice of meat:

1. For best flavor, brown meat slowly on all sides in just enough fat to prevent sticking. Whether to flour first is up to you, although some cooks claim the coating gives the meat a richer color.

2. Add a small amount of liquid—about ½ cup—to start with. You can always add more if it cooks away. Some of the suitable flavor boosters: Broth, bouillon, consommé, vegetable or fruit juices, tomato-juice cocktail or tomato sauce, barbecue sauce, marinades or soups.

3. Cover kettle, frying pan or Dutch oven tightly and simmer (don't boil) or bake in slow oven (325°) until meat is fork-tender.

1553

Know Your ABC's of Cooking Meat

Easiest rule to remember is that the less tender meats are best braised, simmered or stewed. Any of these terms simply means cooking very slowly—either atop the range or in the oven—in liquid such as broth, tomato juice or a tasty sauce. And to bring out the meats' full rich flavor, vary the seasonings.

BEEF ROASTS AND POT ROASTS

WHEN BEEF ROAST IS YOUR CHOICE

Whether it's Dad's favorite to cook on rotisserie or grill, or yours to fix in the oven, a beef roast always makes a hit. Besides the big three—standing and rolled ribs and tenderloin—your supermarket offers many other varieties. Refresher notes here will help you buy the best for the money and occasion.

Know Your Buying Guides

Most of us can pick out firm lean beef well marbled with fat, but these are not the only keys to quality. Other factors that also count are the breed and age of the animal and how it was fed and handled in the packing plant, but this information does not show up at the meat counter. Some homemakers rely on color, but the variation from red to pink, sometimes owing to exposure to air or light, has nothing to do with quality or tenderness.

Your most dependable guide is brand name or grade. As most supermarkets build their reputation on the beef they sell and want you to be a satisfied customer, be loyal once you find a store that gives you the quality and service you want.

What Determines Price?

How much any cut of meat costs depends upon supply and demand, tenderness, and amount of bone, plus the supermarket's charges for trimming, boning and perhaps rolling. If you see a special on a top-quality beef-rib roast, that usually means it is plentiful. Another week a pot roast may be the leader.

If you are comparing prices between supermarkets, consider the same cuts, quality, tenderness and number of servings you will get for your money. The cut with the lowest price per pound is not always your best buy. Generally speaking, rib roasts cost less per pound because they contain the rib bones. All the other choices are boned and trimmed or rolled. And these extra services raise the price.

To show you how to figure costs for yourself, here is an example: A 6-pound bone-in rib roast will yield from 2½ to 3 pounds of boneless cooked meat. If the roast sells for 89¢ a pound, the cost of the edible meat is twice this amount or $1.78 a pound. Compare this to a boneless rolled rib roast at $1.39 a pound with little or no waste or cooking loss and the cooked edible meat weighing about the same as before cooking.

1554

Why Prices Differ on Standing Rib Roasts

Here's where know-how counts, since you'll often find a range in prices. Rib roasts are cut from the center section of the animal between loin and shoulder. The best roast—the one with the highest price tag—is cut nearest the loin and contains the largest rib eye of solid meat. Usually it's called "first cut" or "11th and 12th" rib roast. The largest roasts—6th and 7th ribs—come from the shoulder end of the rib and are often the thriftiest. In between are the center cuts, usually medium-priced.

Another factor affecting price is the length of the rib bone—simply the measure from the tip of the rib to the backbone. For example, a 10-inch rib roast contains long ribs and consequently sells for less. A 7-inch rib is the standard length, although some supermarkets today sell a chunky 6-incher, which means almost all of the short ribs have been trimmed and, therefore, the price will be higher.

How Much to Buy

When you find an attractive "special" on a beef roast, be thrifty and buy two—one to cook now and one to freeze. Or cook both at once and freeze the second for another day.

For best flavor and juicy tenderness, a rib roast should have at least three ribs. This will make four servings with enough left for another meal. In buying a boneless roast, figure four servings per pound.

Store That Roast Right!

Taking care of meat promptly and properly at home is every bit as important as making the right choice at the meat counter. If you plan to hold the roast for one or two days, slit the wrapper, so that air can circulate around the meat, and store it in the coldest part of your refrigerator. If you buy more than you can use within two or three days, freeze it promptly. Unwrap the meat completely, rewrap it in moistureproof paper or foil, seal, label, date and quick-freeze in the coldest part of your freezer.

POPULAR BEEF ROASTS

Although a standing rib rates tops in popularity among all beef roasts, your supermarket has other cuts to suit just about every taste and pocketbook. Every week you may not see all of the leaders, but there will be enough different cuts so you can be choosy.

For indoor or outdoor roasting directions, check your favorite cookbook. And remember: A meat thermometer is a wise investment to help you turn out a juicy, flavorful roast the way you like it best.

Rib Eye—A newcomer, it may be labeled Delmonico in your supermarket. It is the choice meaty center part of a rib roast with outer muscle and all of the bones removed. Look for weights of 3 to 6 pounds, always with a deluxe price.

Eye Round—Because this is solid lean meat covered with a thin layer of fat, it looks like tenderloin, but it's the smallest boneless muscle cut from the animal's leg. For oven-roasting, buy top quality in weights from 2½ to 5 pounds.

Rib—This cut is also called standing rib because the bones form a natural rack to hold the meat upright. Note large "eye" of solid marbled lean covered by a layer of fat. Depending on number of ribs, weights vary from 4 to 10 pounds.

Tenderloin—The most glamorous of all beef roasts—and known as filet mignon when sliced into steaks. It is a long tapering muscle that lies just inside the rib bones. Each weighs from 4 to 6 pounds. Sometimes two come tied together.

Top Round—This is the large, tender, boneless top muscle from the beef leg. It is often cut into a special roast that weighs from 3 to 6 pounds. In shopping, again depend on high quality if you are planning to turn it into an oven roast.

Rolled Rib—Here is the prime rib roast that has been boned, rolled into a plump "log" with an outer covering of fat and neatly tied to hold its compact shape. Most roasts average 4 to 6 pounds. It's an ideal easy-carve show-off for a party.

Sirloin Tip—For hearty roast flavor and neat carving, this lean, boneless, somewhat triangular-shape cut is a favorite. The weight usually ranges from 3 to 5 pounds. If the meat is high quality, it may be oven-roasted to fork tenderness.

Rump Roast—It is oftenest sold as boneless rolled rump, weighing from 4 to 7 pounds. High-quality rump is easy to recognize because of its well-marbled lean. Because of its large size, it is a good choice for planned-over meals.

Prime ribs of beef, roasted to rare perfection and accompanied by butter-sautéed mushrooms and onions.

THE CUTS OF BEEF AND HOW TO COOK THEM

Retail Cuts   *Wholesale Cuts*   *Retail Cuts*

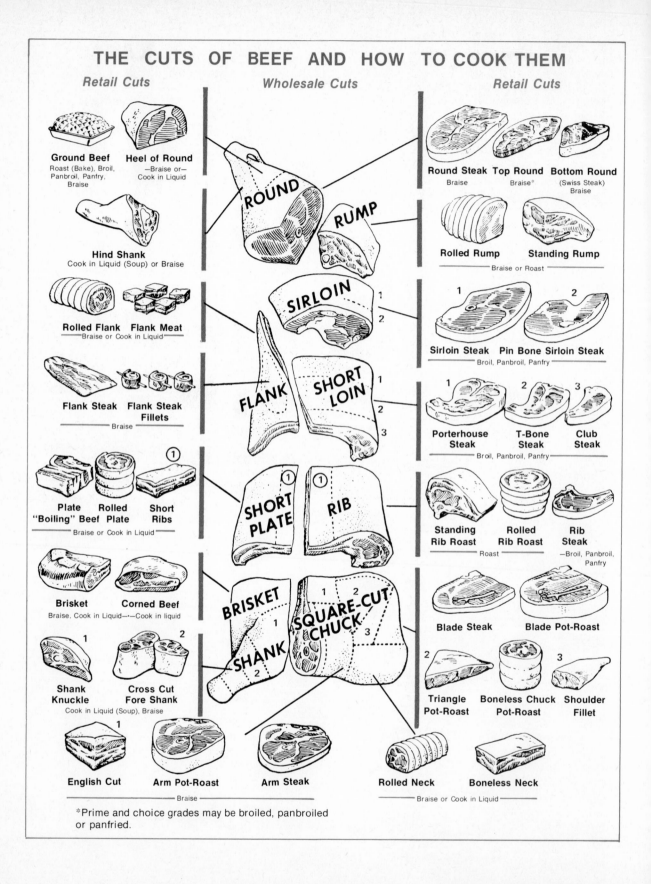

Ground Beef
Roast (Bake), Broil, Panbroil, Panfry, Braise

Heel of Round
—Braise or—
Cook in Liquid

Hind Shank
Cook in Liquid (Soup) or Braise

Rolled Flank   **Flank Meat**
—Braise or Cook in Liquid—

Flank Steak   **Flank Steak Fillets**
—Braise—

Plate   **Rolled**   **Short**
"Boiling" Beef Plate   **Ribs**
—Braise or Cook in Liquid—

Brisket   **Corned Beef**
Braise, Cook in Liquid— —Cook in liquid

Shank Knuckle   **Cross Cut Fore Shank**
Cook in Liquid (Soup), Braise

English Cut   **Arm Pot-Roast**   **Arm Steak**
—Braise—

ROUND

RUMP

SIRLOIN

FLANK

SHORT LOIN

SHORT PLATE

RIB

BRISKET

SHANK

SQUARE-CUT CHUCK

Round Steak   **Top Round**   **Bottom Round**
Braise   Braise*   (Swiss Steak) Braise

Rolled Rump   **Standing Rump**
—Braise or Roast—

Sirloin Steak   **Pin Bone Sirloin Steak**
—Broil, Panbroil, Panfry—

Porterhouse Steak   **T-Bone Steak**   **Club Steak**
—Broil, Panbroil, Panfry—

Standing Rib Roast   **Rolled Rib Roast**   **Rib Steak**
—Roast—   —Broil, Panbroil, Panfry

Blade Steak   **Blade Pot-Roast**

Triangle Pot-Roast   **Boneless Chuck Pot-Roast**   **Shoulder Fillet**

Rolled Neck   **Boneless Neck**
—Braise or Cook in Liquid—

*Prime and choice grades may be broiled, panbroiled or panfried.

Classic Rolled Beef Roast and Oven-Browned Potatoes garnished with peeled wedges of yellow onion.

Classic Rolled Beef Roast

The aristocrat of roasts—and a gem for easy fixing and cooking.

Roast at 325° for 2 to 3 hours. Makes enough for 2 meals, 6 servings each

1 *five-pound boneless sirloin, eye round, rump or chuck roast*
2 *tablespoons all-purpose flour*
1 *teaspoon salt*
¼ *teaspoon pepper*
    PAN GRAVY *(recipe follows)*
    OVEN-BROWNED POTATOES *(recipe follows)*

1 Rub roast all over with mixture of flour, salt and pepper. (If roasting a less tender cut such as eye round, rump or chuck, moisten roast and sprinkle with instant unseasoned meat tenderizer, following label directions.)
2 Place, fat side up, on rack in roasting pan. Do not add water or cover pan. If using a meat thermometer, insert bulb so it reaches center of meat.
3 Roast in slow oven (325°), allowing 20 to 25 minutes per pound or about 2 hours for rare (140°); 30 to 35 minutes or about 3 hours for medium (160°). (If you want to garnish roast with onions, thread peeled onion wedges onto wooden picks and insert into roast for last half hour's cooking.)
4 Remove roast to heated serving platter. (Roast is easier to carve if allowed to stand for 10 to 15 minutes.) Slice and serve with PAN GRAVY and OVEN-BROWNED POTATOES.
5 Wrap leftover meat and chill with leftover gravy for another meal.

    PAN GRAVY—Remove rack from roasting pan. Tip pan and let fat rise in one corner; skim off all fat into a cup, leaving juices in pan. Return 6 tablespoons fat to pan; blend in 6 tablespoons all-purpose flour; cook, stirring all the time, just until mixture bubbles. Stir in 3 cups water

1557

Beefeater's favorite—a lordly prime rib roasted to the peak of perfection and then carved extra-thick.

slowly; continue cooking and stirring, scraping baked-on juices from bottom and sides of pan, until gravy thickens and boils 1 minute. Season to taste with salt and pepper; darken with a little gravy coloring, if you wish. Makes 3 cups.

Oven-Browned Potatoes
Bake at 325° for 1 hour. Makes 6 servings

Pare and quarter 6 medium-size potatoes. Cook in boiling salted water in medium-size saucepan 15 minutes, or until barely tender; drain. Mix 3 tablespoons vegetable oil and 1 teaspoon seasoned salt in baking pan, 13x9x2; arrange potatoes in a single layer in pan. Bake along with roast in slow oven (325°) 30 minutes; turn. Bake 30 minutes longer, or until tender and crusty-golden.

1558

Roast Ribs of Beef
Of all beef cuts, this is the choicest.
Roast at 325° for 3¼ to 4 hours. Makes 12 servings

Buy an oven-ready 3-rib roast, weighing about 10 pounds. Rub well with flour, salt and pepper; place, fat side up, in roasting pan. (Ribs form their own rack.) If using meat thermometer, insert it into meaty center without touching bone. Roast in slow oven (325°), allowing 18 to 23 minutes per pound, or about 3¼ hours for rare (140°); 23 to 28 minutes, or about 4 hours for medium (160°). Remove to a heated serving platter; let stand 10 to 15 minutes for easier carving.

Mushroom-Olive Kebabs
Gay and partylike—and they make a relish-style extra for each plate.

Wash 12 medium-size fresh mushrooms; cut off stems close to caps. With a sharp thin-blade knife, mark center of each cap. Starting here, make a curved cut about ⅛ inch deep to edge. Repeat around cap to make 8 evenly spaced cuts. Now make a second curved cut just behind each line, slanting knife in so you can lift out a narrow strip. (Cap will now spread open slightly when heated.) Heat 2 tablespoons butter or margarine with 1 tablespoon lemon juice in a medium-size frying pan; place mushrooms, cut side down, in pan. Sauté lightly, 1 to 2 minutes, or until golden; turn; sauté 1 minute longer. Thread 2 each, alternately with 2 pitted ripe olives, onto 6 wooden picks; stick a small pickled white onion on end of each pick. Makes 6 kebabs.

Churrasco Roast

Chunky cut of lean beef, spicily marinated, spins to rare perfection on a spit. Recipe makes enough for a bonus meal or two.
Makes about 12 servings

- 1 *rolled boneless sirloin tip, rump or chuck beef roast weighing about 6 pounds*
- 1 *cup wine vinegar*
- ½ *cup olive oil or vegetable oil*
- 3 *tablespoons lemon juice*
- 2 *teaspoons leaf thyme, crumbled*
- 1 *bay leaf*
- 1 *clove of garlic, minced*
- ¼ *teaspoon liquid red pepper seasoning*

1 Place beef in a large shallow pan or roasting pan. Mix remaining ingredients in a 2-cup measure and pour over beef. Cover lightly; chill in refrigerator, turning meat often, 3 to 4 hours.
2 To spit-roast: Remove beef from marinade, saving marinade for basting. Place meat on spit, following manufacturer's directions. If using a meat thermometer, insert bulb in one end of meat. Place spit in position; start rotisserie.
3 Roast, following manufacturer's directions and basting often with marinade, until meat is done as you like it. It will take about 1½ hours for rare, or 140° on meat thermometer. Count on 20 to 30 minutes longer for medium, or 160°.
4 To carve, place on carving board; slice thinly. Serve with juices spooned over.

Rancho Grande Beef Roll

Hot juicy beef sandwiches can't be beat—and what an ideal way to serve a crowd.
Makes 20 servings

Buy an about-5-pound piece of rolled boneless eye round or boned ribs of beef. Rub generously

1559

Another view of prime ribs at their most perfect best. To garnish each plate, a jaunty Mushroom-Olive Kebab.

all over with seasoned salt—about 2 table-spoonfuls. Or buy a rump round or rolled bone-less chuck roast. Omit seasoned salt and instead sprinkle with instant seasoned meat tenderizer, following label directions.

To spit-roast: Place roast on spit, following manufacturer's directions. If using a meat thermometer, insert bulb in one end of meat. Place spit in position; start rotisserie. Roast, following manufacturer's directions, until meat is done as you like it. It will take about 1¼ hours for rare, or 140° on meat thermometer. Count on 20 to 30 minutes longer for medium, or 160°.

To roast on outdoor grill: Place meat on grill over hot coals. Grill, turning often, until it is richly browned on all sides. Continue grilling, turning often, until beef is done as you like it. Time will depend on heat and distance of meat from coals, but it should average about 15 minutes for each pound of meat for rare, about 20 minutes per pound for medium.

To carve: Place on carving board with a well to catch meat juices; slice thinly. Have hot, buttered, toasted split rolls ready to make into sandwiches. Spoon some beef juice over meat.

How to Make the Most of a Chuck Roast:

Here's how to plan two dinners, each deliciously different, plus a soup dividend (from a bone-in cut), from one chuck roast. Because ways of cutting beef vary slightly in different parts of the country, you may find these specials in your supermarket labeled round-bone-arm, blade, California or boneless chuck roast—to name just a few—and each a bargain in beef-dinner meal-planning.

How Much to Buy:

Select an about-3-inch-thick roast with bone, weighing about 5 pounds, or an about-4-pound piece of boneless chuck.

The cut with bone in will have one gener-ous-size lean muscle, A, weighing between 2 and 3 pounds, to cut out for cooking as DEL-MONICO BEEF ROAST. (Use this diagram as a guide.)

1560

The remaining beef, B, depending on the shape of the bone, C, can be sliced for steak or stew. Save the bone for making soup.

It is easy either to slice or cube a boneless chuck, as it is all lean meat. First, slice off a 3-inch-thick piece from the larger end for the roast, then use the remainder for steaks or cubes. No bone, however, so no soup!

Delmonico Beef Roast

A perfect roast for a small family. It carves beautifully with no waste.
Roast at 325° about 2 hours. Makes 6 servings

This lean boneless section will weigh 2 to 3 pounds and can be roasted with flour, salt and pepper rubbed into it, or tenderized with seasoned or unseasoned meat tenderizer, following label directions. Tie roast to hold its round shape. (If using meat thermometer, insert bulb through side into center of cut.) Place roast on a rack in small roasting pan; roast in slow oven (325°), allowing about 40 minutes per pound if you like beef pink to medium, with lots of juice. (Thermometer should register about 150°.)

If your range has only one oven, bake YORK-SHIRE PUFFS *(recipe follows)* along with the roast this easy way. Thirty minutes before meat is done, remove it from oven; reset oven regulator to hot (400°). Spoon enough hot drippings from pan to grease cups generously. (Drippings help to flavor puffs, too.) Have batter ready and divide among cups; place in a shallow pan for easy handling and slide into oven. Return beef to oven; bake 30 minutes. Take out beef; let puffs bake 20 minutes longer. During the last 20 minutes you will have time to make gravy, if you wish, and complete rest of meal. Roast will carve better when allowed to sit for this time. Transfer roast to carving board and slice with a sharp knife across the grain.

BEEF PAN GRAVY—Tip roasting pan and let fat rise in one corner; skim off all but 2 tablespoons. Blend in 2 tablespoons all-purpose flour; stir in 1½ cups water. Cook, stirring and scraping baked-on juices from bottom and sides of pan, until gravy thickens slightly and boils 1 minute. Season to taste with salt and pepper; stir in a little gravy coloring, if you wish. Makes 1½ cups.

Yorkshire Puffs

You can serve these golden Yorkshire-pudding puffs and gravy, too, with your beef roast.
Bake at 400° for 50 minutes. Makes 8 popover puffs.

3 eggs
1 cup milk
1 cup sifted all-purpose flour
½ teaspoon salt

1 Beat eggs slightly with rotary beater in bowl

or 4-cup measure; add milk, flour and salt; beat briskly ½ minute; scrape side of bowl; beat 1½ minutes longer. Batter will be smooth and thin.

2 Grease 8 small custard cups (deep straight-side cups let puffs pop higher) with beef drippings from roast, or butter cups well. Divide batter evenly among them, filling about ⅓ full. Place, evenly spaced, in pan and set on oven shelf in back of roast or on shelf above it.

3 Bake in hot oven (400°) 30 minutes (popovers will have puffed enough to hold their shape when you open oven door); take out roast. Bake puffs 20 minutes longer, or until richly golden. (If baking puffs separately, there's no need to peek at them while they're baking.)

Note—To keep puffs crisp and hot if they must wait a few minutes before serving, take from cups, make a small slit in the side of each to let steam escape. Place in pan and put back into hot oven with heat turned off and door open.

●

Easiest-Ever Pot Roast
So little fixing needed here, and only a whit of watching as the meat cooks.
Makes 6 servings

1 boneless beef rump or chuck pot roast, weighing about 4 pounds
1 envelope instant meat marinade
1 can (12 ounces) mixed vegetable juices
1 bag (2 pounds) frozen mixed vegetables for stew
1 envelope mushroom gravy mix
½ cup water

1 Place meat in a kettle or Dutch oven; pierce all over with a fork.

2 Stir meat marinade into ⅔ cup of the vegetable juices in a 1-cup measure; pour over meat. Let stand at room temperature, turning meat several times, 15 minutes. Pour remaining vegetable juices into kettle; cover.

3 Heat to boiling, then simmer, turning meat several times, 2 hours. Arrange frozen vegetables around meat; heat to boiling again. Simmer 1½ hours longer, or until meat and vegetables are very tender.

4 Remove all to a heated serving platter; keep hot while making gravy.

5 Pour liquid into a 4-cup measure; let stand a few minutes, or until fat rises to top, then skim off. Add water, if needed, to make 3 cups; return liquid to kettle. Stir mushroom-gravy mix into

Good roast beef dinner companions: asparagus spears drizzled with butter, snowy cauliflower, sliced carrots.

the ½ cup water in a cup; stir into liquid in kettle. Heat slowly, stirring constantly, to boiling, then cook 5 minutes, or until gravy thickens.
6 Carve meat into ¼-inch-thick slices. Serve with vegetables and gravy to spoon over all.

Pot Roast Seville

Rings of colorful stuffed olives dot each slice. For a subtly different flavor, gravy calls for a secret ingredient.
Makes 6 servings

    1 round, rump, or boneless chuck beef roast, weighing about 4 pounds
    1 jar (about 5 ounces) stuffed small Spanish olives
    1 medium-size onion, chopped (½ cup)
    1 jar (about 5 ounces) baby-pack strained carrots
    1 cup water
    1 tablespoon instant coffee powder
    1 tablespoon sugar
    1 teaspoon salt
    ¼ teaspoon pepper
    ½ cup light cream or table cream
    2 tablespoons all-purpose flour

1 Make slashes about 1½ inches deep and 2 inches apart all the way around meat with a sharp knife; push an olive deep into each cut.
2 Brown beef in its own fat in a Dutch oven over medium heat or in an electric skillet; remove and set aside.
3 Sauté onion until soft in same pan; stir in carrots, water, instant coffee, sugar, salt and pepper. Return meat to pan; cover.
4 Simmer, turning meat once or twice, 3 hours, or until very tender. Remove to a heated serving platter; keep hot while making gravy.
5 Pour liquid into a 2-cup measure; let stand about a minute, or until fat rises to top. Skim off fat, then measure 2 tablespoonfuls back into pan. Add cream, plus water if needed, to liquid to make 2 cups.
6 Blend flour into fat in pan; cook, stirring constantly, just until bubbly. Stir in the 2 cups liquid; continue cooking, stirring constantly, until gravy thickens and boils 1 minute.
7 Carve meat into ¼-inch-thick slices; serve with gravy and saffron rice, if you wish.
Note—To fix saffron rice, crush about 3 strands of saffron and stir into cooking water for rice. For 6 servings of 1 cup each, you will need 1½ cups uncooked rice.

Australian Beef Roast

Five vegetables cook mealy and brown along with roast, take on its meaty richness.

Australian Beef Roast is actually a one-dish dinner.

Roast at 325° about 2 hours. Makes enough for 2 meals, 4 servings each

4 medium-size parsnips, pared, sliced lengthwise and cut into 3-inch lengths
4 medium-size onions, peeled
4 medium-size potatoes, pared and halved
4 medium-size carrots, scraped and cut diagonally into 2-inch strips
1 large acorn squash, quartered and seeded
6 pounds boneless beef rump or round
 Unseasoned instant meat tenderizer
2 tablespoons vegetable oil
4 tablespoons all-purpose flour

1 Prepare all vegetables. Parboil parsnips and onions together; and potatoes, carrots and squash together in boiling salted water in 2 large kettles 15 minutes. Drain, saving 3 cups potato liquid for Step 6.
2 Moisten roast and sprinkle with meat tenderizer, following label directions. Place on rack in large shallow roasting pan. (If using a meat thermometer, insert bulb into center of roast.) Arrange vegetables in separate piles around the meat; brush lightly with vegetable oil.
3 Roast in slow oven (325°), allowing about 20 minutes per pound if you like beef pink with lots of juice. (Thermometer should register 140°.) During roasting, turn vegetables and baste once or twice with drippings in pan. Vegetables and roast should be done at the same time.
4 Remove roast to heated platter; arrange vegetables around edge. Keep hot while making gravy.
5 Remove rack from pan; tip pan and let fat rise to one corner; skim off all fat. Return 4 tablespoons to pan; blend in flour; stir in saved 3 cups potato liquid. Cook, stirring and scraping baked-on juices from bottom and sides of pan, until gravy thickens and boils 1 minute. Season to taste with salt and pepper; darken with a few drops gravy coloring, if you wish. Makes 3 cups.

**Barbecued Pot Roast with
Golden Dumplings**
Cornmeal puffs steam fluffy and light in the tomato-rich sauce after meat is done.
Makes 6 servings

1 round, rump or boneless chuck beef roast, weighing about 4 pounds
1 large onion, chopped (1 cup)
1 clove garlic, minced

1 can (1 pound) tomatoes
¼ cup firmly packed brown sugar
2 teaspoons salt
1 teaspoon Italian seasoning
¼ teaspoon pepper
3 tablespoons cider vinegar
1 tablespoon prepared mustard
1 tablespoon Worcestershire sauce
3 tablespoons all-purpose flour
 GOLDEN DUMPLINGS (recipe follows)

1 Brown beef in its own fat in a Dutch oven over medium heat or in an electric skillet; remove and set aside.
2 Sauté onion and garlic until soft in same pan; stir in tomatoes, brown sugar, salt, Italian seasoning, pepper, vinegar, mustard and Worcestershire sauce. Return meat to pan; cover.
3 Simmer, turning meat once or twice, 3 hours, or until very tender. Remove to a heated serving platter; keep hot while making gravy and GOLDEN DUMPLINGS.
4 Pour liquid into a 4-cup measure; let stand about a minute, or until fat rises to top. Skim off fat, then measure 3 tablespoonfuls back into pan. Add water, if needed, to liquid to make 3 cups.
5 Blend flour into fat in pan; cook, stirring constantly, just until bubbly. Stir in the 3 cups liquid; continue cooking, stirring constantly, until gravy thickens and boils 1 minute.
6 Mix GOLDEN DUMPLINGS. Drop batter in 6 mounds into bubbling hot gravy; cover. Cook, without peeking, 20 minutes. (Dumplings will be puffed and light.)
7 Arrange around meat on platter; carve meat into ¼-inch-thick slices; serve with gravy.
 GOLDEN DUMPLINGS—Combine ¾ cup all-purpose sifted flour, 2 teaspoons baking powder, 1 teaspoon salt and ½ cup cornmeal in a medium-size bowl. Combine ⅔ cup milk and 2 tablespoons vegetable oil in a 1-cup measure; stir into dry ingredients just until mixture is moist. (Dough will be soft.)

Pot Roast Pacifica
Orange juice blends with tomato, herbs and spice for the tantalizing seasoner.
Makes 6 servings

1 blade-bone chuck beef roast, weighing about 4 pounds
2 tablespoons lemon juice
6 slices bacon, diced
1 medium-size onion, chopped (½ cup)
1 clove garlic, minced
1½ cups orange juice
1 cup diced peeled ripe tomato (1 large)
1 tablespoon sugar

1563

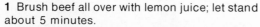

3 teaspoons salt
1 teaspoon leaf thyme, crumbled
½ teaspoon ground nutmeg
¼ teaspoon pepper
1 bay leaf
3 tablespoons cornstarch
¼ cup water

1 Brush beef all over with lemon juice; let stand about 5 minutes.
2 Sauté bacon with onion and garlic until bacon is crisp in a Dutch oven or an electric skillet; remove and set aside.
3 Brown beef in bacon drippings in same pan over medium heat; stir in bacon mixture, orange juice, tomato and seasonings; cover.
4 Simmer 3 hours, or until meat is very tender. Remove to a heated serving platter; keep hot while making gravy.
5 Pour liquid into a 4-cup measure; let stand about a minute, or until fat rises to top. Skim off fat and remove bay leaf. Add water, if needed, to liquid to make 3 cups; return to pan; heat to boiling.
6 Blend cornstarch with water in a cup; stir into hot liquid. Cook, stirring constantly, until gravy thickens and boils 3 minutes.
7 Carve meat into ¼-inch-thick slices; serve with gravy.

Pot Roast Kun Koki

Plan ahead when serving this savory roast, as meat seasons in a soy-sesame sauce for several hours before cooking.
Makes 6 servings

2 tablespoons sesame seeds
1 cup water (for meat)
¼ cup soy sauce
2 tablespoons molasses
2 tablespoons wine vinegar or cider vinegar
2 green onions, chopped
1 teaspoon garlic powder
⅛ teaspoon cayenne
1 round, rump or boneless chuck beef roast, weighing about 4 pounds
2 tablespoons cornstarch
2 tablespoons water (for gravy)

1 Toast sesame seeds in a small frying pan over low heat, shaking pan often, just until golden-brown.
2 Combine seeds with the 1 cup water, soy sauce, molasses, vinegar, green onions, garlic powder and cayenne in a 2-cup measure; pour

over meat in a large bowl; cover. Chill, turning meat several times to season evenly, 3 to 4 hours, or overnight.
3 When ready to cook, remove meat from the marinade, then pat dry. Brown in its own fat in a Dutch oven over medium heat or in an electric skillet; pour marinade over; cover.
4 Simmer, turning meat once or twice, 3 hours, or until very tender. Remove to a heated serving platter; keep hot while making gravy.
5 Pour liquid into a 2-cup measure; let stand about a minute, or until fat rises to top. Skim off fat. Add water, if needed, to liquid to make 2 cups; return to pan; heat to boiling.
6 Blend cornstarch with the 2 tablespoons water in a cup; stir into hot liquid. Cook, stirring constantly, until gravy thickens and boils 3 minutes.
7 Carve meat into ¼-inch-thick slices; serve with gravy.

Rio Roast

Budget-smart pot roast seasons in an herb-spice marinade before cooking.
Makes 6 servings

4 pounds blade chuck roast, cut about 2 inches thick
1 cup wine vinegar or cider vinegar
½ cup vegetable oil
2 cloves of garlic, minced
1 tablespoon chili powder
1 tablespoon leaf marjoram, crumbled
2 teaspoons leaf thyme, crumbled
2 teaspoons salt
1 bay leaf

1 Place roast in a shallow glass or plastic dish. Mix remaining ingredients in a small bowl; pour over meat; cover. Chill, turning meat several times, 4 hours to season.
2 When ready to cook, lift meat from marinade, letting excess drip back into dish. Pat meat dry with paper toweling.
3 Brown slowly in its own fat in a large frying pan; cover.
4 Cook over low heat, turning once or twice, 1½ hours, or until tender. (No need to add any liquid as marinade steams out as meat cooks.)
5 Remove to carving board or heated serving platter; slice and serve with pan juices.

Sicilian Beef Dinner

Makes 8 servings, plus enough for a bonus meal

1 rolled rump beef roast, weighing about 4 pounds
3 tablespoons vegetable oil

1564

Sicilian Beef Dinner: rolled rump smothered with tomatoes, spiked with garlic and surrounded with pasta.

"Roast" beef in a skillet? Why not? It works magnificently with Country Skillet Beef, a heady recipe heightened with red pepper rings and sliced zucchini.

1 large onion, chopped (1 cup)
1 tablespoon parsley flakes
1½ teaspoons leaf oregano, crumbled
1 teaspoon leaf basil, crumbled
1 teaspoon salt
½ teaspoon instant minced garlic
¼ teaspoon seasoned pepper
1 can (about 2 pounds) Italian tomatoes
1 cup water
1 package (8 ounces) shell macaroni
2 tablespoons all-purpose flour

1566

1 Brown roast slowly in vegetable oil in a kettle or Dutch oven. Add onion, parsley flakes, oregano, basil, salt, garlic, pepper, tomatoes and ½ cup of the water to kettle. Heat to boiling; cover.

2 Simmer, turning meat several times, 2¾ hours, or until tender. Remove from kettle to a large deep serving platter.

3 While roast simmers, cook macaroni, following label directions; drain.

4 Blend flour with remaining ½ cup water until smooth in a cup; stir into liquid in kettle. Cook,

stirring constantly, until sauce thickens and boils 1 minute. Season with salt, if needed.

5 Remove strings from roast; slice meat ¼ inch thick. Spoon macaroni shells around meat; spoon part of the sauce over macaroni. Garnish platter with watercress, if you wish. Serve remaining sauce separately.

●

Beef Agrigento
The unusual flavor comes from a secret ingredient—anchovy paste.
Makes 8 servings, plus enough for a bonus meal

1 round, rump or boneless chuck beef roast, weighing 4 to 5 pounds
2 tablespoons vegetable shortening
2 tablespoons sugar
1 teaspoon salt
1 teaspoon whole allspice
6 peppercorns
1 large onion, chopped (1 cup)
1 clove of garlic, minced
1 bay leaf

1 can (10½ ounces) condensed beef broth
1 tube (2 ounces) anchovy paste
2 tablespoons cider vinegar
⅓ cup sifted all-purpose flour
1 cup light cream or table cream

1 Brown roast slowly in shortening in a Dutch oven or electric skillet.
2 Stir in sugar, salt, allspice, peppercorns, onion, garlic, bay leaf, beef broth, anchovy paste and vinegar. Heat to boiling; cover.
3 Simmer, turning meat once or twice, 3 hours, or until very tender. Remove to a heated platter; keep warm.
4 Strain liquid into a 4-cup measure. Let stand several minutes, or until fat rises to top, then skim off; measure ⅓ cupful and return to Dutch oven. Add water to liquid, if needed, to make 4 cups.
5 Blend flour into fat in Dutch oven; cook, stirring constantly, just until bubbly. Stir in the 4 cups liquid; continue cooking and stirring until gravy thickens and boils 1 minute. Stir in cream; heat very slowly.
6 Carve part of the meat into ¼-inch-thick slices. Serve with gravy, and lightly buttered cooked spaghetti, if you wish. Wrap remaining meat and chill for another meal.

Country Skillet Beef
The all-time old-time favorite—simmered with simple spices to savory perfection.
Makes enough for 2 meals, 4 to 6 servings each

6 to 7 pounds beef blade or round-bone chuck roast
1 medium-size onion, sliced
½ cup water
1 teaspoon salt
6 peppercorns
1 bay leaf
4 to 6 medium-size potatoes, pared and halved
4 to 6 small zucchini, sliced
1 sweet red pepper, sliced in rings
3 tablespoons all-purpose flour

1 Brown beef in its own fat in large heavy kettle, Dutch oven or frying pan; remove and set aside. Drain all but 2 tablespoons fat from kettle.
2 Sauté onion until softened in same kettle; add water and seasonings. Return meat to kettle; cover.
3 Simmer 2 hours, or until meat is almost tender. Lay potatoes around meat; cover; simmer 30 minutes. Arrange zucchini on top of meat; cover; simmer 15 minutes. Add pepper rings; simmer 10 minutes longer, or until vegetables are tender.

4 Remove meat and vegetables to heated platter; keep hot.
5 Strain broth into a 4-cup measure, pressing onion through sieve; let stand about a minute, or until fat rises to top. Skim off fat and return 3 tablespoons to kettle; blend in flour. Add water to broth, if needed, to make 3 cups; stir into flour mixture in kettle. Cook, stirring constantly and scraping cooked-on juices from bottom and sides of pan, until the gravy thickens and boils 1 minute.
6 Slice meat; serve with vegetables, and gravy to spoon over.
7 Wrap any leftover meat; chill meat and leftover gravy for another meal.

Savory Beef Pot Roast
Succulent and juicy, and a favorite with most men.
Makes 6 servings

4 pounds boneless pot roast (chuck, round, or rump)
1 tablespoon drippings
3 large onions, sliced
1½ teaspoons salt
½ teaspoon leaf thyme, crumbled
¼ teaspoon pepper
1 can (6 ounces) tomato paste
½ cup water

1 Brown meat in drippings in large heavy kettle or Dutch oven; add remaining ingredients; cover tightly.
2 Simmer 2 to 2½ hours, or until meat is fork-tender. Add a little water during cooking, if needed. Remove meat to heated serving platter; keep hot while making gravy.
3 Strain liquid through sieve, pressing onions through. Let stand until fat rises to top; skim; measure liquid, then return to kettle and heat to boiling. For each 1 cup of liquid, blend 1 tablespoon flour with 1 tablespoon cold water in cup to make a smooth paste; stir into hot liquid. Cook, stirring constantly, until gravy thickens and boils 1 minute; season with salt and pepper to taste.

1567

El Rancho Roast
Pungent ripe olives and mild cinnamon give this roast a tantalizingly subtle flavor.
Makes enough for 2 meals, 4 to 6 servings each

5 to 6 pounds beef round, rump, sirloin tip or boneless chuck roast

1 can (6 ounces) tomato paste
1 cup sliced pitted ripe olives
¼ cup water
2 tablespoons lemon juice
1 tablespoon sugar
2 teaspoons salt
1 teaspoon ground cinnamon
½ teaspoon pepper
3 tablespoons all-purpose flour

1 Brown meat in its own fat in large heavy kettle or Dutch oven; mix remaining ingredients, except flour, in a small bowl; pour over meat; cover.
2 Simmer 2½ to 3 hours, or until meat is very tender. Remove to heated serving platter; keep hot while making gravy.
3 Pour liquid into a 4-cup measure; let stand about a minute, or until fat rises to top; skim off fat and return 3 tablespoons to kettle; blend in flour. Add enough water to liquid to make 3 cups; stir into flour mixture. Cook, stirring constantly and scraping cooked-on juices from bottom and sides of pan, until gravy thickens and boils 1 minute.
4 Slice meat; serve with gravy to spoon over. A big panful of hot corn bread makes a scrumptious go-with.
5 Wrap any leftover meat; chill meat and leftover gravy for another meal.

Spanish Beef Roast

As you slice this savory roast, neat cuts of stuffed green olives pop out.
Bake at 325° for 3 hours. Makes enough for 2 meals, 4 to 6 servings each

5 to 6 pounds beef, round, rump, sirloin tip or boneless chuck roast
1 jar (about 5 ounces) stuffed green olives
4 tablespoons all-purpose flour
1 Spanish onion, sliced thin
1 smoked sausage or frankfurter, sliced thin
1 can (12 ounces) mixed vegetable juices
1 teaspoon salt
¼ teaspoon liquid red pepper seasoning

1 Make slashes about 1½ inches deep and 2 inches apart with a sharp knife all the way around meat; push an olive into each cut until it disappears.
2 Rub beef well with flour; brown in its own fat in large heavy kettle or Dutch oven; remove and set aside. Drain all but 2 tablespoons fat from kettle.

3 Sauté onion just until softened in same kettle; stir in and brown sausage or frankfurter slices. Stir in vegetable juices, salt and red pepper seasoning; return meat to kettle; cover.
4 Bake in slow oven (325°) 3 hours, or until meat is very tender. Remove to heated serving platter; keep hot.
5 Let gravy stand about a minute, or until fat rises to top; skim. (Gravy will have thickened slightly with flour from roast.) Reheat just to boiling.
6 Slice meat; serve with hot gravy to spoon over. Potatoes—either hashed brown or made into a hot potato salad—are an inviting accompaniment to this exotic roast.
7 Wrap any leftover meat; chill meat and leftover gravy for another meal.

●

Jumbo Roast with Spaghetti

Zesty tomato sauce both seasons the meat and makes a generous topping for spaghetti.
Baked at 325° for 3 hours. Makes enough for 2 meals, 4 to 6 servings each

6 to 7 pounds beef blade or round-bone chuck roast
4 tablespoons all-purpose flour
1 large onion, chopped (1 cup)
1 clove of garlic, minced
1 can (about 2 pounds) Italian tomatoes
1 can (3 or 4 ounces) sliced mushrooms
1 tablespoon mixed Italian herbs
2 teaspoons salt
1 teaspoon sugar
½ teaspoon leaf oregano, crumbled
Buttered hot spaghetti

1 Rub beef well with flour; brown in its own fat in large heavy kettle or Dutch oven; remove and set aside.
2 Sauté onion and garlic until softened in same kettle; stir in tomatoes, mushrooms and liquid and seasonings; heat to boiling. Return meat to kettle; cover.
3 Bake in slow oven (325°) 3 hours, or until meat is very tender. Remove to heated serving platter; keep hot.
4 Let sauce stand about a minute, or until fat rises to top; skim. Reheat just to boiling; spoon part over spaghetti; serve with roast.
5 Wrap any leftover meat; chill meat and leftover sauce for another day.

1568

Viennese Boiled Beef
Makes 8 servings

- 1 beef rump roast (about 5 pounds)
- 1 medium-size onion, halved
- 2 medium-size carrots, pared and sliced (1 cup)
- 1 stalk of celery, sliced
- 1 bay leaf
- 1 teaspoon salt
- ½ teaspoon peppercorns
  COLD HORSERADISH SAUCE (recipe follows)

1 Place beef in a kettle or Dutch oven; add onion, carrot, celery, bay leaf, salt, peppercorns and water just to cover meat; heat to boiling; reduce heat; cover. Simmer 3 hours, or until meat is fork-tender.
2 Place beef on a carving board; slice. Serve on a heated platter, accompanied by COLD HORSE-RADISH SAUCE. (If you wish, strain broth; refrigerate. Use for a vegetable soup or gravy base.)

COLD HORSERADISH SAUCE—Combine ½ cup fresh bread crumbs, ¼ cup milk, 2 tablespoons prepared horseradish and ¼ teaspoon salt; let stand about 15 minutes, or until bread crumbs are soft. Beat ½ cup cream for whipping until stiff in a small bowl; fold in horseradish mixture; refrigerate until ready to serve. Makes 2 cups.

Ukrainian Kettle
Makes 8 servings

- 1 bottom round beef roast (about 4 pounds)
- 2 tablespoons vegetable oil
- 1 large onion, diced (1 cup)
- 2 teaspoons seasoned salt
- 1 teaspoon seasoned pepper
- 1 can (10½ ounces) condensed beef broth
- 2 small yellow turnips (about 2½ pounds)
- 1 cup sliced celery

1 Brown meat on all sides in oil in a kettle or Dutch oven. Add onion, seasoned salt and pepper and beef broth. Heat to boiling; reduce heat; cover. Simmer 2 hours.
2 Pare turnips; cut into 1-inch cubes. Add with celery to meat, turning to coat with liquid in kettle. Cover; simmer 1 hour longer, or until meat and vegetables are tender.
3 Place pot roast on a carving board; cut into thick slices; arrange on a platter. Remove vegetables from kettle with a slotted spoon and ar-

range around meat. Spoon cooking liquid over all. Or, use cooking liquid to prepare a gravy, (recipe follows).

GRAVY—Pour cooking liquid into a 2-cup measure; add water, if needed, to make 2 cups; return to kettle and bring to boiling. Blend ¼ cup sifted all-purpose flour with ¼ cup water in a jar with a tight-fitting lid; shake to mix well; stir into boiling liquid. Cook, stirring constantly, until gravy thickens and bubbles 1 minute. Pour a little gravy over the meat and serve the remainder separately.

Old German Sauerbraten
Plan this favorite days ahead, as it should season in a spicy marinade before cooking.
Makes enough for 2 meals, 4 to 6 servings each

- 5 to 6 pounds beef round, rump, sirloin tip or boneless chuck roast
- 2 cups wine vinegar or cider vinegar
- 2 cups water
- ¼ cup firmly packed brown sugar
- 1 tablespoon salt
- ½ teaspoon pepper
- ½ teaspoon ground cloves
- 1 bay leaf
- 3 medium-size onions, chopped (1½ cups)
- 2 large carrots, diced (1½ cups)
- 1½ cups diced celery
- 2 tablespoons bacon drippings or vegetable shortening
- 8 gingersnaps, crumbled

1 Place meat in a large bowl; pour mixture of vinegar, water, brown sugar, seasonings and vegetables over. Cover; store in refrigerator 2 to 3 days, turning meat several times to marinate on all sides.
2 When ready to cook, remove meat from marinade and pat dry; brown in hot drippings or shortening in large heavy kettle or Dutch oven; add vegetables from marinade, and liquid to a depth of 1 inch.
3 Cover kettle tightly; simmer 3 hours, or until meat is very tender. Remove to heated serving platter; keep hot while making gravy.
4 Strain broth into a 4-cup measure; let stand about a minute, or until fat rises to top. Skim off fat, returning 4 tablespoons to kettle.
5 Add water to broth, if needed, to make 2 cups; stir back into kettle; sprinkle crumbled gingersnaps over. Cook, stirring constantly, until gravy thickens and is bubbly-hot.

1569

6 Slice meat; serve with gravy to spoon over. Go-withs for this Old World specialty: Freshly boiled potatoes in their jackets and steamed cabbage wedges sprinkled with caraway seeds.

●

Bavarian Beef Dinner
Comes to the table, like sauerbraten, with potato pancakes, gravy and sweet-sour red cabbage. Makes 8 servings, plus enough for a bonus meal

1 round, rump or boneless chuck beef roast, weighing 4 to 5 pounds
2 tablespoons vegetable shortening
1 tablespoon sugar
3 teaspoons salt
2 teaspoons caraway seeds
½ teaspoon ground cardamom
1 large onion, chopped (1 cup)
1 large carrot, pared and chopped (1 cup)
1 cup sliced celery
½ cup chopped parsley
1 cup dry red wine

1 Brown roast slowly in shortening in a Dutch oven or electric skillet.
2 Stir in sugar, salt, caraway seeds, cardamom, onion, carrot, celery, parsley and wine; heat to boiling; cover.
3 Simmer, turning meat once or twice, 3 hours, or until very tender. Remove to a heated serving platter; keep warm while making gravy.
4 Spoon liquid from Dutch oven into an electric-blender container; cover; beat until smooth. (Or strain into a bowl, pressing vegetables through sieve into liquid.) Return liquid to Dutch oven and reheat just to boiling.
5 Carve part of the meat into ¼-inch-thick slices. Top with several spoonfuls of gravy. Serve with remaining gravy.

●

Beef 'n' Kraut Platter
Caraway-seeds, paprika and onion season the meat an Old World way. Creamy sauerkraut serves as "sauce" and vegetable go-with. Makes 6 servings

1571

1 round, rump or boneless chuck beef roast, weighing about 4 pounds
1 cup water
¼ cup chili sauce
1 envelope or can (2 to a package) onion-soup mix
1 tablespoon caraway seeds
1 tablespoon paprika

Cardamom-and-caraway-scented Bavarian Beef Dinner.

Counting pennies? Try succulent Glazed Corn Beef, glazed ham-style with brown sugar and zippy mustard.

¼ teaspoon pepper
1 can (1 pound, 11 ounces) sauerkraut, drained
¼ cup firmly packed brown sugar
1 cup (8-ounce carton) dairy sour cream

1 Brown beef in its own fat in a Dutch oven over medium heat or in an electric skillet; stir in water, chili sauce, onion-soup mix, caraway seeds, paprika and pepper; cover.
2 Simmer, turning meat once or twice, 2 hours; skim off all fat. Mix sauerkraut and brown sugar in a medium-size bowl; stir into liquid around meat; cover again. Simmer 1 hour longer, or until meat is very tender. Remove to a carving board; keep hot while finishing sauce for sauerkraut.
3 Stir about ½ cup of the hot sauerkraut mixture into sour cream in a medium-size bowl, then stir back into remaining sauerkraut mixture in pan. Heat *very slowly* just until hot. (Do not boil.)
4 Spoon sauerkraut into a deep serving platter. Carve meat into ¼-inch-thick slices; place on top of sauerkraut. Serve with buttered noodles, if you wish.

Brisket Dinner
Beef, four vegetables and rich brown gravy make this meal-on-a-platter. And everything cooks together.
Makes 6 servings

1 fresh beef brisket, weighing about 3 pounds
1 cup water
2 envelopes instant beef broth
   OR: 2 beef-bouillon cubes
1 clove garlic, minced
1 bay leaf
1 medium-size onion, peeled
8 whole cloves
12 small white onions, peeled
6 medium-size carrots, scraped and cut in 2-inch pieces
6 medium-size parsnips, scraped and cut in 2-inch pieces
2 teaspoons salt
¼ teaspoon pepper
6 large fresh mushrooms
3 tablespoons all-purpose flour

1 Brown beef in its own fat in a Dutch oven over medium heat or in an electric skillet; stir in water, beef broth or bouillon cubes, garlic and bay leaf. Stud onion with cloves; drop into pan; cover.
2 Simmer, turning meat once, 1½ hours. Place small onions, carrots and parsnips around meat, turning in liquid in pan to coat; sprinkle with salt and pepper; cover again.

3 Simmer 45 minutes; add mushrooms. Simmer 15 minutes longer, or until meat and vegetables are tender.
4 Remove meat to a heated serving platter; place vegetables around edge, discarding onion with cloves and bay leaf; keep hot while making gravy.
5 Pour liquid into a 4-cup measure; let stand about a minute, or until fat rises to top. Skim off fat, then measure 3 tablespoonfuls back into pan. Add water, if needed, to liquid to make 3 cups.
6 Blend flour into fat in pan; cook, stirring constantly, just until bubbly. Stir in the 3 cups liquid; continue cooking, stirring constantly, until gravy thickens and boils 1 minute.
7 Carve meat into ¼-inch-thick slices; serve with gravy.

Glazed Corned Beef
It's good budgeting and planning to buy a big piece of corned beef—enough for two meals.
Makes about 12 servings

1 piece corned beef brisket (about 5 pounds)
10 peppercorns
1 bay leaf
¼ teaspoon leaf thyme, crumbled
2 tablespoons brown sugar
1 teaspoon dry mustard

1 Simmer meat with peppercorns, bay leaf and thyme in water to cover in large kettle 3½ to 4 hours, or until tender. Let meat stand in its broth until ready to serve, then reheat, if needed.
2 Place meat, fat side up, on carving board or platter; sprinkle top evenly with a mixture of brown sugar and mustard. (Sugar melts and glazes meat as it stands.)
3 Slice thin across the grain; serve with mustard-pickle relish.
4 Chill any remaining meat to slice another day for a cold-cut or sandwich meal, or to grind for corned-beef hash.

1573

VEAL

WHAT YOU SHOULD KNOW ABOUT VEAL

Most of us don't know veal as well as we ought. It's a European favorite, but we Americans prefer the more robust flavor and texture of beef.
   Beef, of course, is simply "veal grown up,"

Veal isn't a meat Americans dote upon as much as beef. But it is meltingly tender when roasted to perfection.

because veal comes from very young calves, those between one and three months old. The meat is exceedingly delicate and should be cooked with tender loving care.

TIPS ON BUYING VEAL:

Look for Quality: Most of the veal sold in supermarkets bears the U.S. Department of Agriculture shield-shaped grade stamp: USDA PRIME, CHOICE and GOOD are the three top grades; CHOICE and GOOD are those you're most likely to see. The meat will also bear the round federal inspection stamp if it has been sold in interstate commerce, meaning that it has been inspected and found to be wholesome.

Sometimes, certain cuts do not show the grade stamp so it's good to learn to recognize top-quality veal simply by looking at it. Ideally, veal should be delicate pink in color (sometimes it's pale, pale gray-pink) with velvety, finely grained flesh. There should be very little fat within the lean—*marbling,* this is called—and what outer covering of fat there is should be firm and snowy white.

Learn the Cuts: Because veal is infant beef, its cuts are very much like those of beef—only smaller. The following chart will help you to identify the cuts and indicate how each is best prepared.

How Much to Buy? Figure on ½ pound bone-in veal roast for each serving and ¼ to ⅓ pound for a boned and rolled roast. If you're planning a crown roast, simply allow one to two chops per person.

THE CUTS OF VEAL AND HOW TO COOK THEM

Retail Cuts   *Wholesale Cuts*   *Retail Cuts*

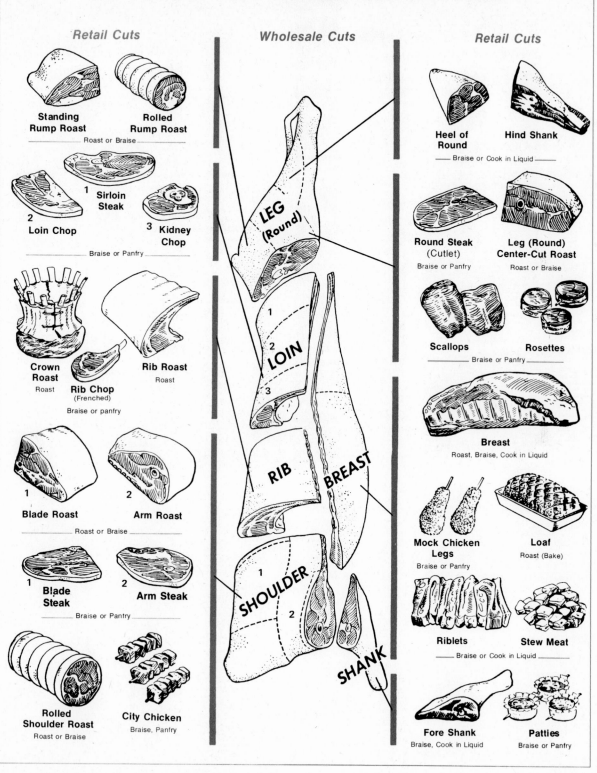

Standing Rump Roast   **Rolled Rump Roast**
—— Roast or Braise ——

2 Loin Chop   **1 Sirloin Steak**   **3 Kidney Chop**
—— Braise or Panfry ——

Crown Roast
Roast   **Rib Chop** (Frenched)   **Rib Roast**
Roast
Braise or panfry

1 Blade Roast   **2 Arm Roast**
—— Roast or Braise ——

1 Blade Steak   **2 Arm Steak**
—— Braise or Pantry ——

Rolled Shoulder Roast
Roast or Braise

City Chicken
Braise, Panfry

LEG (Round)

LOIN

RIB

SHOULDER

BREAST

SHANK

Heel of Round   **Hind Shank**
—— Braise or Cook in Liquid ——

Round Steak (Cutlet)
Braise or Panfry   **Leg (Round) Center-Cut Roast**
Roast or Braise

Scallops   **Rosettes**
—— Braise or Panfry ——

Breast
Roast, Braise, Cook in Liquid

Mock Chicken Legs
Braise or Panfry   **Loaf**
Roast (Bake)

Riblets   **Stew Meat**
—— Braise or Cook in Liquid ——

Fore Shank
Braise, Cook in Liquid   **Patties**
Braise or Panfry

ROASTS, JUICY AND TENDER

VEAL—TENDER LEAN MEAT FROM YOUNG CALVES

Rump of veal is a generous cut that can be used in many ways. Because veal is lean and mild-tasting, it blends perfectly with richer foods such as bacon, salt pork, cheese and sour cream. Its bone is small, but it's well worth taking the time to simmer it in salted water, as the flavorful broth it makes is wonderful for cooking vegetables such as carrots, onions and green beans.

How to Divide a Veal Roast

A 4- to 5-pound rump roast will provide both a roast and enough thin slices (scallops) for another meal. Its shape, tapered at one end, full and flat at the other *(see sketch below)*, makes it simple to cut up.

Starting at full end, A, cut off 4 slices, each about ½ inch thick. Pounding later will flatten and even them out. These will weigh about 1 pound. Slicing will expose the hipbone, B, making it easy to cut around and remove it. All that is left, C, is solid meat—3 to 4 pounds—for a gorgeous roast.

Paprika Veal Roast

It's a cut of solid meat—tender as chicken. Delicious eating cold, too.
Roast at 325° about 2 hours. Makes 6 servings

    3 to 4 pounds boned rump of veal
    1 large onion, sliced
    ½ teaspoon salt
    ½ teaspoon paprika
    ⅛ teaspoon pepper
    ½ pound fat salt pork, cut into ½-inch-wide
      strips
      LEMON PARSLEY NOODLES (recipe follows)

1 Fill cavity from blade bone with onion slices; fold meat over; hold in shape with skewers or string. Rub all over with mixture of salt, paprika and pepper.
2 Crisscross salt-pork strips over top, fastening with wood picks to hold in place. Place meat on rack in small roasting pan. (If using a meat thermometer, insert so bulb reaches meaty center.)

3 Roast in slow oven (325°), allowing 30 minutes per pound, or about 2 hours for a 4-pound cut. (Thermometer should register 180°.) Cut away strings on roast. Use drippings for LEMON PARSLEY NOODLES.

Lemon Parsley Noodles

Veal gravy, zipped with lemon and parsley, adds a delightful flavor to noodles.

Cook 1 package (8 ounces) noodles, following label directions; drain. While noodles cook, strain and measure drippings from PAPRIKA VEAL ROAST pan; add enough water to make 1 cup. Stir 1 tablespoon flour into pan, then add drippings mixture. Cook over low heat, stirring constantly, until gravy thickens and boils 1 minute. Stir in ½ teaspoon grated lemon peel; season to taste with salt and pepper. Toss with drained noodles; sprinkle with 2 tablespoons chopped parsley. Makes 6 servings.

Onion-Herb Veal Roast

Dip mix from an envelope gives this roast its crusty coating and savory flavor.
Roast at 325° for 2 to 3 hours. Makes enough for 2 meals, 6 servings each

    1 envelope (about 1 tablespoon) onion dip mix
    3 tablespoons all-purpose flour
    2 tablespoons vegetable oil
    1 five-pound rump of veal roast
      CREAM GRAVY (recipe follows)

1 Smooth dip mix, flour and vegetable oil to a paste in cup; spread evenly over meat.
2 Place on rack in roasting pan. Do not add water or cover pan. If using a meat thermometer, insert bulb so it reaches center of meat without touching bone.
3 Roast in slow oven (325°), allowing 30 minutes per pound, or about 2½ hours. Thermometer should register 180°.
4 Remove meat to heated serving platter. Slice and serve with CREAM GRAVY.
5 Wrap leftover meat and chill for another meal.
CREAM GRAVY—Remove rack from roasting pan. Tip pan and let fat rise in one corner; skim off all fat into a cup, leaving juices in pan. Return 2 tablespoons fat to pan; blend in 2 tablespoons all-purpose flour, ½ teaspoon salt and ⅛ teaspoon pepper; cook, stirring all the time, just until mixture bubbles. Stir in 1 cup water slowly; continue cooking and stirring, scraping baked-on juices from bottom and sides of pan, until gravy thickens and boils 1 minute; remove from heat. Blend in 1 cup dairy sour cream, then heat slowly 1 to 2 minutes, but do

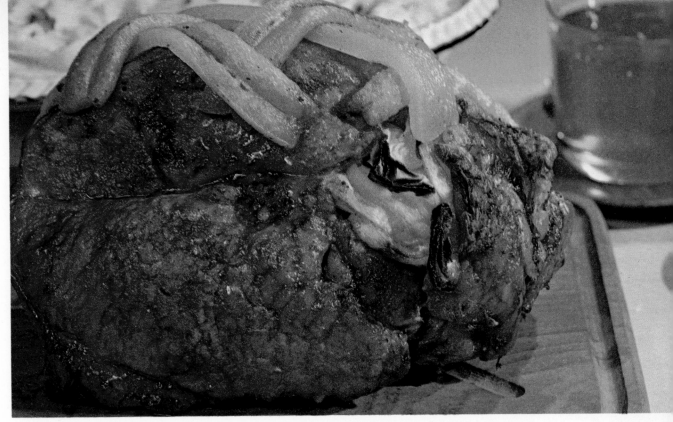

Paprika Veal Roast, festooned with lardoons of fat salt pork, is so tender it cuts at the touch of a fork.

not let gravy boil, as it may curdle. Makes about 2 cups.

●

Veal Fricandeau
One of the most popular Continental ways with veal. Meat is roasted with bacon, then served with a sparkly gravy.
Roast at 325° for 1 hour and 30 minutes. Makes 2 meals, 2 servings each

  1 three-pound rump of veal roast, boned
10 slices bacon
    BROWN CREAM GRAVY (recipe follows)

1 Top roast with bacon slices, overlapping slightly; tie with string. If using a meat thermometer, insert bulb into center of roast.
2 Roast in slow oven (325°) about 1½ hours, or until thermometer registers 180°.
3 Remove to platter; keep hot while making gravy. Cut string from roast but leave bacon in place; carve into ¼-inch-thick slices.
    BROWN CREAM GRAVY—Strain drippings into a 1-cup measure; let fat rise to top, then skim off; measure 1 tablespoonful back into pan. Add milk to liquid to make 1 cup. Blend 1 tablespoon all-purpose flour into fat in pan; cook, stirring constantly, just until bubbly. Stir in the 1 cup

drippings mixture; continue cooking and stirring until gravy thickens and boils 1 minute. Stir in 1 tablespoon currant jelly; season to taste with salt and pepper. Makes 1 cup.

●

Veal Roast Italiano
Makes 8 servings

  1 bone-in veal rump roast (about 5 pounds)
  1 can (1 pound) stewed tomatoes
  2 cloves of garlic, sliced
  3 teaspoons salt
  1 packaged bouquet garni
  1 eggplant, about 1½ pounds
  1 package (9 ounces) frozen artichoke hearts
  1 cup frozen whole mushrooms (from a 10-ounce package)
  1 pound spaghetti
  2 tablespoons butter or margarine
 ½ cup water
 ½ cup sifted all-purpose flour

1577

1 Trim any excess fat from meat; brown on all sides in a kettle or Dutch oven. Add tomatoes, garlic, 2 teaspoons of the salt and the bouquet garni. Heat to boiling; reduce heat; cover. Simmer 1½ hours.
2 Trim and dice eggplant (do not pare); add

to kettle; stir in artichoke hearts, mushrooms and remaining 1 teaspoon salt; cover. Simmer 1 hour longer, or until meat and vegetables are tender.

3 Cook spaghetti, following label directions; drain; toss with butter or margarine; keep warm.

4 Place meat on a carving board; keep warm. Remove vegetables from kettle with a slotted spoon to a bowl; keep warm.

5 Bring sauce in kettle to boiling. Blend water with flour in a jar with a tight-fitting lid; shake to mix well. Stir into boiling sauce. Cook, stirring constantly, until sauce thickens and bubbles 1 minute. Return vegetables to sauce; heat just to bubbling.

6 To serve, spoon spaghetti onto deep platter; pour sauce over spaghetti. Carve meat into thick slices and arrange around spaghetti.

Savory Veal Roll

Simmer meat in a spicy sauce, then serve with horseradish gravy.
Makes 6 servings

3 to 4 pounds rolled boned veal shoulder
6 tablespoons all-purpose flour
1 tablespoon dry mustard
1 tablespoon brown sugar
2 teaspoons salt
1 teaspoon poultry seasoning
⅛ teaspoon pepper
2 tablespoons vegetable oil
1 large onion, chopped (1 cup)
¼ cup chopped celery
2 tablespoons chopped parsley
2 tablespoons cider vinegar
½ cup water
2 teaspoons prepared horseradish

1 Rub veal well with mixture of 2 tablespoons flour, mustard, brown sugar, salt, poultry seasoning and pepper. (Save remaining flour for gravy in Step 5.)

1578

2 Brown meat slowly in vegetable oil in heavy kettle or Dutch oven. Add onion, celery, parsley and vinegar; cover.

3 Simmer 2½ hours, or until meat is tender. Remove to carving board or heated serving platter; keep hot.

4 Strain stock into a 2-cup measure; let fat rise to top; skim off all fat. Add water to stock, if needed, to make 2 cups; return to kettle.

5 Smooth saved 4 tablespoons flour to a paste with water in a cup; stir into stock in kettle. Cook, stirring all the time, until gravy thickens and boils 1 minute. Stir in prepared horseradish.

Braised Stuffed Breast of Veal

A wonderful way to prepare this low-cost meat—delightfully stuffed, braised and sauced.
Makes 8 servings

1 boned breast of veal (about 2¼ pounds)
¾ teaspoon salt
⅛ teaspoon pepper
2 tablespoons chopped parsley
½ teaspoon leaf basil, crumbled
½ pound sausage meat (from a 1 pound package)
1 cup grated carrots (about 3 large carrots)
1 tablespoon butter or margarine
½ cup sliced celery
1 medium-size onion, sliced
1 can (about 14 ounces) chicken broth
Water
3 tablespoons flour

1 Spread breast of veal flat on a cutting board. (It should measure about 8 inches by 15 inches.) Sprinkle with salt, pepper, parsley and basil. Combine sausage meat with grated carrots in a small bowl; spread evenly over surface of veal, pressing firmly. Roll up veal from short end, jelly-roll fashion. Tie crosswise with heavy string at 1½-inch intervals.

2 Brown meat in butter or margarine in Dutch oven; add celery and onion; sauté 5 minutes longer. Add chicken broth; simmer, covered, 2 hours, or until meat is tender. Remove meat to a carving board.

3 Strain pan juices through a sieve; press vegetables through; pour into a 2-cup measure; add water if necessary to make 1¾ cups. Return to Dutch oven.

4 Combine flour and 6 tablespoons water in a 1-cup measure; blend until smooth. Pour into juices in Dutch oven. Cook, stirring constantly, until sauce thickens and bubbles 3 minutes.

5 Remove string from veal; cut into thin slices; serve with vegetable sauce.

Veal à la Mode

One-dish dinner—veal and vegetables simmered in a seasoned apple broth.
Makes 8 servings

1 rolled boned veal shoulder, weighing 4 to 5 pounds
2 tablespoons vegetable shortening
1 envelope onion-flavor salad dressing mix
1 cup apple juice
16 small white onions, peeled

2 medium-size potatoes, pared and cubed (2 cups)
2 large carrots, pared and sliced (2 cups)
2 medium-size parsnips, pared and sliced (2 cups)
1 can (6 ounces) sliced mushrooms
3 tablespoons all-purpose flour

1 Brown veal slowly in shortening in a Dutch oven or electric skillet.
2 Sprinkle with salad dressing mix; stir in apple juice. Heat to boiling; cover.
3 Simmer, turning meat once or twice, 1 hour. Add onions; simmer 30 minutes. Add potatoes, carrots and parsnips. Simmer 30 minutes longer, or until meat and all vegetables are tender. Remove meat to a cutting board; keep warm while making gravy.
4 Drain liquid from mushrooms into a cup; add mushrooms to other vegetables. Blend flour into mushroom liquid until smooth; stir into vegetable mixture.
5 Cook, stirring constantly, until mixture thickens and boils 1 minute. Spoon onto a heated deep platter.
6 Carve meat into ¼-inch-thick slices; arrange over vegetables. Serve with thick slices of crusty bread, if you wish.

Ballotine de Veau
Makes 8 servings

1 breast of veal, weighing about 5 pounds
½ pound ground veal
½ pound ground lean pork
¼ cup chopped parsley
1 tablespoon chopped onion
4 teaspoons salt
¾ teaspoon leaf tarragon, crumbled
½ teaspoon ground nutmeg
¼ teaspoon pepper
2 tablespoons dry sherry
2 tablespoons cream for whipping
1 ham steak, cut ¼ inch thick and weighing about ¼ pound
¼ cup chopped pistachio nuts
    Bones from breast of veal
2 carrots, pared and quartered
2 medium-size onions, peeled and quartered
2 bay leaves
2 stalks celery with leaves, cut up
8 peppercorns
    RED-WINE SAUCE (recipe follows)

1 Have your meatman bone veal and wrap bones with meat to use for making broth.
2 Combine ground veal, pork, parsley, chopped onion, 1 teaspoon of the salt, tarragon, nutmeg, pepper, sherry and cream in a large bowl; mix lightly until well blended.
3 Open breast of veal out flat on counter top; spread ground-meat mixture evenly over veal to within 1 inch of edges. Cut ham into ½-inch-wide strips; place lengthwise in rows over stuffing; sprinkle pistachio nuts over ham.
4 Fold edges of veal breast up over filling to cover completely; sew edges and ends of meat together with heavy thread. Wrap roll in wet double-thick cheesecloth; tie ends tightly, then tie roll in several places to hold during cooking. Place roll in a deep large roasting pan. (If your pan is not large enough to hold roll in one piece, cut it in half; wrap each half tightly in cheesecloth. Place halves, side by side, in pan.)
5 Add veal bones, remaining 3 teaspoons salt, carrots, onion quarters, bay leaves, celery and peppercorns to roasting pan; pour in enough water to cover roll. Heat to boiling; cover. Simmer 2 hours, or until veal is tender.
6 Remove to a cutting board; cut away strings and cheesecloth. Carve roll into thick slices with a very sharp knife; pull out thread. Serve meat with RED-WINE SAUCE. (Strain broth and chill to use for soup another day.)

RED-WINE SAUCE—Sauté 2 tablespoons finely chopped onion in 4 tablespoons (½ stick) butter or margarine until soft in a small saucepan; blend in 4 tablespoons all-purpose flour. Cook, stirring constantly, until bubbly. Stir in 2 envelopes instant beef broth or 2 teaspoons granulated beef bouillon and 1¾ cups water; continue cooking and stirring until sauce thickens and boils 1 minute. Stir in ¼ cup dry red wine. Makes about 2 cups.

LAMB

LAMB ROASTS: WISE BUYS AT ANY PRICE

1579

Leg of lamb is No. 1 in popularity, but there are many runner-up roasts that promise top value for your money. Notes here, plus the photo-guide that follows will help you identify four leading choices—two for company occasions and two for pennywise family meals.

TIPS ON BUYING LAMB

Experienced homemakers remember when the term ''spring lamb'' was heard every year. Then it meant that this choice meat was available only during March, April and May. Today

Crown Roast of Lamb stuffed with ground lamb and rice.

When Is the Price Right?

The price at any time depends on quality, amount of bone and waste and current supply, and it pays to consider all of these factors. For example, leg of lamb will be most in demand and its price tag will reflect this. Crown roast or rack of lamb, both specially made from the rib sections, will always carry deluxe prices. Bone-in roasts cost less per pound than the same cuts boned and rolled, as these extra services take time and know-how. If your budget's in a squeeze, check the shoulder roasts or lamb breast—both thrifty, but as flavorful, juicy and easy to fix as costlier cuts.

How Much to Buy?

As an overall guide, figure on ½ pound bone-in leg or shoulder roast for each serving and ¼ to ⅓ pound for a boned rolled roast. If a crown roast or rack fits your menu plan best, it's easiest to count noses and allow 1 or 2 chops for each person.

Buy with an Eye on Savings:

Lamb on special? Be economical and buy a whole leg weighing from 5 to 8 pounds, then turn it into three different meals. Here's how: Ask your meatman to cut off several 1-inch-thick steaks from the sirloin end and a generous piece from the shank end. What's left in the middle makes an ideal small roast. Broil the steaks, cube the shank meat for stew or curry, and roast the center for Sunday dinner.

POPULAR LAMB ROASTS

Leg—Shown is a whole leg with tailbone (V-shape section), part of hipbone (at wide end) and long leg bone. Sometimes end of leg or shank bone is cracked and folded under. For smaller roasts, some stores sell half legs, labeled "shank half" or "sirloin half," or simply "leg of lamb." Full legs average 5 to 8 pounds.
Boneless Rolled Shoulder—A budget buy, it's actually square-cut shoulder that has been boned, rolled and tied. Weighs from 2½ to 6 pounds. Leg, sirloin and breast are also sold boneless.
Rack of Lamb—Luxury roast of rib chops left in one piece with backbone removed for easy carving. Depending on number of ribs, it weighs from 3 to 5 pounds.
Square-Cut Shoulder—Note the square shape with layers of lean and fat and some bone. It's an economical choice weighing 4 to 6 pounds, and is easier to carve into chunks than into slices.

the phrase means little. Some lamb shows up on meat counters the year round, although, like many foods, it still has its peak season. Most animals go to market when they're less than a year old, and their meat is lean, tender and tops in flavor. Take care, when you buy, not to confuse lamb with mutton, which comes from more mature animals, usually 1½ to 2 years old.

When You Shop:

Most large supermarkets carry lamb, but not all will have it every day nor will they necessarily advertise it. When it's important to have what you want when you want it, order ahead. At other times, be flexible and simply jot down "lamb" on your shopping list. Then, when you get to the store, look over what's there and pick the cut that fits your purpose and pocketbook.

Whatever cut of lamb you buy, look for pink-to-reddish lean meat with a fine velvety texture and waxy-white, smooth, firm fat. The outer fat will be covered with a natural pink paper-thin skin called "fell" that helps the meat hold its shape and juiciness during cooking. For highest quality, always check for a U. S. Government grade of PRIME or CHOICE, a meat packer's grade, or the supermarket's own brand.

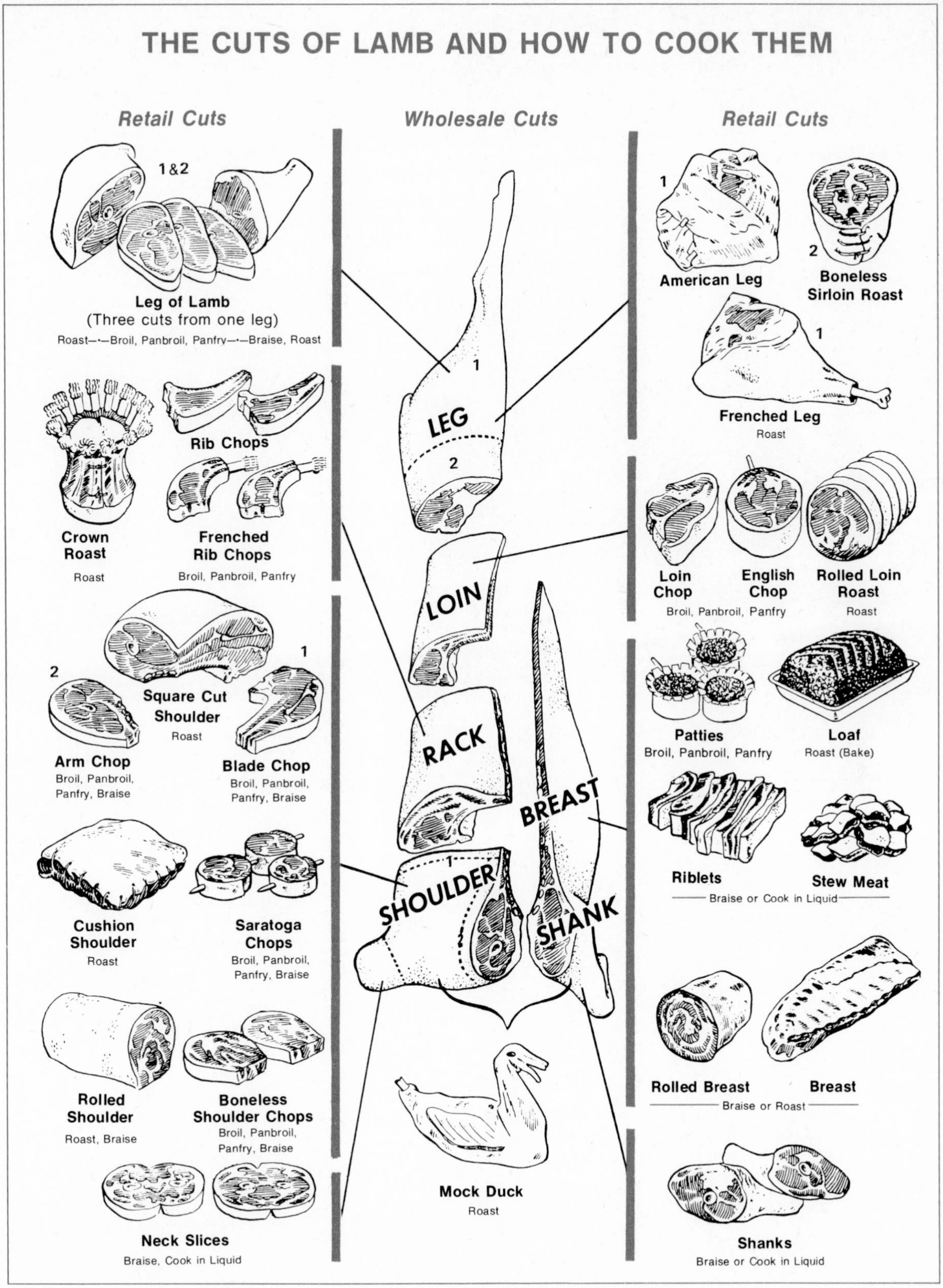

THE CUTS OF LAMB AND HOW TO COOK THEM

Retail Cuts	*Wholesale Cuts*	*Retail Cuts*

1 & 2

Leg of Lamb
(Three cuts from one leg)
Roast—•-Broil, Panbroil, Panfry—•-Braise, Roast

LEG

American Leg

Boneless Sirloin Roast

Frenched Leg
Roast

Rib Chops

Crown Roast
Roast

Frenched Rib Chops
Broil, Panbroil, Panfry

LOIN

Loin Chop

English Chop

Rolled Loin Roast
Roast
Broil, Panbroil, Panfry

Square Cut Shoulder
Roast

Arm Chop
Broil, Panbroil, Panfry, Braise

Blade Chop
Broil, Panbroil, Panfry, Braise

RACK

Patties
Broil, Panbroil, Panfry

Loaf
Roast (Bake)

Cushion Shoulder
Roast

Saratoga Chops
Broil, Panbroil, Panfry, Braise

BREAST

SHOULDER

SHANK

Riblets

Stew Meat
— Braise or Cook in Liquid —

Rolled Shoulder
Roast, Braise

Boneless Shoulder Chops
Broil, Panbroil, Panfry, Braise

Mock Duck
Roast

Rolled Breast

Breast
— Braise or Roast —

Neck Slices
Braise, Cook in Liquid

Shanks
Braise or Cook in Liquid

Cumberland Lamb Roast, decorated with thinnest lemon slices, glistening under its currant jelly glaze.

Crown Roast of Lamb

Order roast ahead and ask your meatman to grind the trimmings for stuffing.
Roast at 325° about 2 hours. Makes 8 servings

1 sixteen-chop crown lamb roast
1 pound ground lamb (from trimmings)
1 large onion, chopped (1 cup)
1 can (3 or 4 ounces) sliced mushrooms
1 teaspoon salt
1 teaspoon leaf rosemary, crumbled
2 cups cooked rice

1 Place crown roast, rib ends up, in a large shallow baking pan; remove ground lamb from center of roast. (If using a meat thermometer, insert bulb into meaty portion of one chop without touching bone.)
2 Shape ground lamb into a patty in a large frying pan; brown 5 minutes on each side, then break up into chunks; remove with a slotted spoon to a large bowl. Pour all drippings from pan, then measure 2 tablespoonfuls and return to pan.

3 Stir onion into frying pan; sauté until soft. Stir in mushrooms and liquid, salt and rosemary; add to lamb with rice; toss lightly to mix.
4 Cut a strip of foil 12 inches wide and long enough to go around roast with a slight overlap; fold lengthwise into a 4-inch-wide strip. Wrap tightly around bone edge of roast to hold in stuffing. Spoon stuffing into center of roast, mounding slightly. Cover with another piece of foil to prevent over-browning.
5 Roast in slow oven (325°) 2 hours, or until meat is richly browned. (Thermometer should register 170° for pinky-medium or 180° for well done.)
6 Lift roast carefully onto a carving board or heated serving platter with two pancake turners. For a holiday-bright garnish, arrange rings of cooked carrot slices and peas inside bone edge of roast. Slice two preserved kumquats; stand slices, petal fashion, in center of roast; spoon mint jelly in center. Arrange watercress around roast, if you wish.
7 To serve, start in center of stuffing and cut between ribs into wedges.

1582

Cumberland Lamb Roast

A Sunday-dinner roast, especially inviting for Easter. Tart currant jelly glazes the meat to a rich sparkle.
Roast at 325° for 2½ to 3 hours. Makes 6 servings, plus enough for another meal and soup

    1 leg of lamb, weighing 6 to 7 pounds
    1 teaspoon salt
    1 teaspoon dry mustard
    ½ teaspoon ground ginger
    5 thin lemon slices
    ⅔ cup currant jelly
    1 tablespoon lemon juice
      CUMBERLAND GRAVY (recipe follows)

1 Trim excess fat from lamb. Rub lamb well with mixture of salt, mustard and ginger. Place, rounded side up, on a rack in roasting pan. If using meat thermometer, stick it into the thickest meaty part without touching bone. Do not cover pan.
2 Roast in slow oven (325°) 2 hours. Remove from oven.
3 Cut 4 of the lemon slices in half; arrange the 8 half slices petal fashion on side of roast, holding in place with dampened wooden picks; place the whole slice in center.
4 Break up jelly with a fork in a cup; stir in lemon juice; spread over lamb. Return to oven.
5 Continue roasting ½ to 1 hour longer, or until thermometer registers 170° for pinky-medium, 180° for well done.
6 Remove to heated serving platter; pull out wooden picks from lemon garnish before carving roast. Keep hot while making gravy.
  CUMBERLAND GRAVY—Remove rack from roasting pan. Tip pan and pour off all fat, leaving drippings in pan. Return ½ cup fat to pan. Blend in ½ cup sifted all-purpose flour, 1½ teaspoons salt and ¼ teaspoon pepper; cook, stirring constantly, just until mixture bubbles. Stir in 4 cups water; continue cooking and stirring, scraping baked-on juices from bottom and sides of pan, until gravy thickens and boils 1 minute. Makes 4 cups.

TWO GOURMET DINNERS FROM A LEG OF LAMB:

With a meals-ahead plan, you can have two completely different main dishes and a flavorful dinner soup from a 7- to 8-pound leg of lamb.

How to Divide the Cut:

Learn to be your own meat cutter (it's simple to follow this sketch) and it will put pennies back into your food budget, give you completely different meals from one cut. Here's how with a leg of lamb:

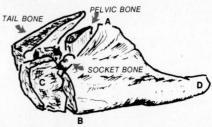

Starting at A, cut deeply with sharp thin longblade knife into meat along near side of pelvic bone until you reach small round ball and flat socket bone. Next, at B, cut straight into meat to socket-bone cut. Continue to cut through meat to sever piece C for kebabs. (It will have pelvic and tail bones attached.) Now cut away meat from bones, using meat for BLUE-PLATE LAMB KEBABS and saving bones for soup. The round socket bone will protrude slightly from one end of leg to be roasted. If leg has a shank bone, twist it and cut off at D for soup.
  Shank end of leg, weighing about 5 pounds, is now ready for LA CIENEGA LAMB ROAST. Recipes follow.

La Cienega Lamb Roast

A special flavor secret is in its buttery crust coating.
Roast at 325° about 2½ hours. Makes 6 servings

    ½ leg of lamb (about 5 pounds)
      Salt and pepper
    3 tablespoons all-purpose flour
    2 tablespoons bottled garlic spread
      LAMB PAN GRAVY (recipe follows)

1 Sprinkle lamb all over with salt and pepper. Make a paste of flour and garlic spread in a cup; spread evenly over meat. Place meat on rack in roasting pan. (If using a meat thermometer, insert bulb so it reaches meaty center without touching bone.)
2 Roast in slow oven (325°), allowing 30 minutes per pound, or about 2½ hours. (Thermometer should register 175° for medium, or 182° for well done.) Place roast on heated platter while making gravy.
  LAMB PAN GRAVY—Tip roasting pan and let fat rise in one corner; skim off all but 2 tablespoons. Blend in 2 tablespoons all-purpose flour; stir in 2 cups water. Cook, stirring and scraping down baked-on juices from bottom and sides of pan, until gravy thickens slightly and boils 1 minute. Season to taste with salt and pepper; stir in a little gravy coloring, if you wish. Makes 2 cups.

1583

For La Cienega Lamb Roast, a leg of lamb is blanketed with a crispy brown flour crust flavored with garlic.

Peach Savories

An accompaniment of golden fruit with a chutneylike flavor.
Makes 6 servings

1 can (about 1 pound) cling peach halves
1 tablespoon bottled savory sauce
1 teaspoon cider vinegar
⅛ teaspoon salt

1 Combine peaches and syrup with remaining ingredients in medium-size frying pan. Simmer, turning peaches once, 5 minutes.
2 Let stand at least 30 minutes to season, or make a day ahead and chill. Delicious eating, warm or cold.

Blue-Plate Lamb Kebabs

Cubes of seasoned lamb on one skewer, vegetables on another make this fancy save-a-little dish.
Makes 6 servings

30 small cubes of lamb, cut from hip end of
leg (about 1½ pounds)
½ cup vegetable oil
¼ cup cider vinegar
1 teaspoon salt
½ teaspoon dillweed
OR: ½ teaspoon leaf rosemary or marjoram, crumbled
½ teaspoon pepper
6 medium-size carrots, scraped and cut into
1-inch chunks
1 package (10 ounces) frozen Brussels sprouts
PEANUT PILAF (recipe follows)

1 Place lamb cubes in single layer in·shallow pan.
2 Combine vegetable oil, vinegar, salt, herb and pepper in 1-cup measure; pour over lamb; let stand, turning meat once or twice, at least 2 hours, or chill overnight.
3 Cook carrots and Brussels sprouts in ½-inch depth of slightly salted water in separate small saucepans, allowing 10 minutes for carrots and 5 minutes for the sprouts, or just until crisply tender; drain.

4 Thread marinated lamb cubes onto 6 individual skewers; alternate carrots and sprouts on 6 more skewers; brush all with lamb marinade.
5 Broil lamb and vegetables, brushing often with marinade, 4 to 5 minutes on each side, or until done as you like them.
6 Arrange alternate lamb and vegetable skewers on a bed of hot PEANUT PILAF on heated platter, or serve individually.

Peanut Pilaf
Tastes scrumptiously gourmetlike.
Makes 6 servings

1 cup uncooked regular rice
2 cups water
½ teaspoon salt
1 teaspoon grated onion
1 tablespoon butter or margarine
2 chicken-bouillon cubes
¼ teaspoon ground ginger
¼ cup chopped dried apricots
¼ cup chopped salted peanuts

1 Combine rice, water, salt, onion, butter or margarine, bouillon cubes and ginger in medium-size saucepan; heat to boiling, stirring with a fork to mix well.

2 Cover; simmer about 15 minutes, or until rice is tender and liquid is absorbed.
3 Stir in apricots and peanuts; fluff lightly with fork.

Killarney Lamb Roast
Homemade lemon "marmalade" glazes and seasons the meat to perfection.
Roast at 325° for 3½ to 4 hours. Makes 8 servings, plus enough for another meal

1 leg of lamb, weighing 8 to 9 pounds
3 teaspoons salt
1 teaspoon ground nutmeg
¼ teaspoon cayenne
1 medium-size lemon
½ cup sugar
1 can (6 ounces) frozen concentrate for lemonade
  Water
3 tablespoons all-purpose flour
1 bunch fresh mint, washed and dried

1 Trim excess fat from lamb. Rub lamb well with mixture of salt, nutmeg and cayenne. Place roast, rounded side up, on a rack in a shallow roasting pan. If using a meat thermometer, in-

1585

Blue-Plate Lamb Kebabs are cut from the tender leg, marinated with dill and rosemary, broiled quickly, then arrayed upon a bed of Peanut Pilaf.

sert bulb into thickest meaty part without touching bone. Do not cover pan or add water.

2 Roast in slow oven (325°) 2 hours, or until thermometer registers 150°; remove from oven.

3 While meat roasts, pare peel from lemon in thin shreds, then pare white membrane from fruit; section fruit.

4 Combine sectioned fruit and peel with sugar and concentrate for lemonade in a large saucepan; heat slowly, stirring constantly, until sugar dissolves, then cook, stirring often, 7 minutes, or until slightly thickened. Spoon part over lamb.

5 Continue roasting, basting every 20 minutes with remaining lemon mixture, 1½ hours, or until thermometer registers 170° for pinky-medium. If you prefer lamb well done, continue roasting to 180°. Remove roast to a heated large serving platter and take out thermometer; keep meat hot while making gravy.

6 Remove rack from roasting pan. Pour all fat and drippings into a 2-cup measure; let stand a minute, or until fat rises to top, then skim off and discard. Add water to drippings to make 2 cups; return to pan. Blend flour with another 1 cup water until smooth; stir into pan. Cook, stirring constantly and scraping baked-on juices from bottom and sides of pan, until gravy thickens and boils 1 minute.

7 Garnish lamb platter with mint and lemon roses, if you wish. Carve meat into ¼-inch-thick slices; serve with gravy. (To make lemon roses: Choose medium-size fruit, and, starting at the blossom end of each, pare off peel in one continuous long strip. Wind strip round and round to form a rose pattern.)

Broiled Leg of Lamb
Makes 8 servings

1586

    1 leg of lamb weighing about 7 pounds,
      boned and butterflied
    1 cup dry red wine
    ½ cup orange juice
  1¼ cups water
    3 tablespoons vegetable oil
    2 tablespoons chili sauce
    2 cloves garlic, crushed
    1 teaspoon salt
    ¾ teaspoon leaf oregano, crumbled
    ⅛ teaspoon pepper
    1 large onion, sliced
    2 teaspoons firmly packed brown sugar
    ¼ cup sifted all-purpose flour

1 Trim all fat from meat. Combine wine, orange juice, ¼ cup of the water, vegetable oil, chili sauce, garlic, salt, oregano and pepper in a large shallow glass dish; add sliced onion. Place lamb in marinade, turning to coat well; cover. Chill, turning meat occasionally, 12 hours or overnight.

2 Remove lamb from marinade; place on rack of broiler pan and let stand at room temperature for 1 hour before broiling. Strain marinade into a bowl. Stir in remaining 1 cup water and the brown sugar.

3 Preheat broiler. Broil lamb, 6 inches from heat, turning about every 10 minutes, for 50 minutes.

4 Carve; thicker parts will be pink inside and thin ones well done.

5 Stir flour into the pan drippings; cook, stirring constantly, just until bubbly. Stir in marinade; continue cooking and stirring until gravy bubbles 1 minute.

Broiled Lamb Parisienne
Be the first of your group to serve lamb this way. Meat is boned, then seasoned—both fix-ahead jobs—before quick-cooking.
Makes 8 servings

    1 leg of lamb, weighing about 7 pounds
    ⅔ cup olive oil or vegetable oil
    3 tablespoons lemon juice
    1 envelope old-fashioned French salad-dressing mix
      SKILLET TOMATO BOUQUETS (recipe follows)

1 Order the lamb ahead and ask your meatman to bone it or do it yourself with a sharp-tip thin-blade knife this way: Starting at the top end and working with the point of the knife in short strokes, cut meat from bone. Work carefully, pulling away meat from bone as you go, so you'll know where to cut. When you reach the joint, twist bone to remove. Then go to shank end and remove shank bone the same way.

2 To remove remaining bone, cut through meat at the thinnest point, then peel back meat and remove bone. (It will be shaped like a dumbbell.) Meat will be uneven in thickness, but this doesn't matter. Save the bones to simmer for making soup; trim all fat from meat and discard.

3 Mix olive oil or vegetable oil, lemon juice and salad-dressing mix in a large shallow glass dish; place lamb in marinade, turning to coat well; cover. Chill, turning meat every few hours, 12 hours, or even overnight, to season.

4 About ½ hour before serving time, remove lamb from marinade and place on rack in broiler pan.

5 Broil, 6 inches from heat, 15 minutes; turn.

Killarney Lamb Roast sparkles underneath a homemade lemon marmalade made in jig time with frozen lemonade.

Broil 15 minutes longer, or until richly browned and crispy at edges.

6 Place on a cutting board; carve into ¼-inch-thick slices. (Thicker parts will be pink inside and thin ones well done.) Serve with SKILLET TOMATO BOUQUETS.

Skillet Tomato Bouquets
Rosy whole tomatoes topped with mushrooms, olives and mint make this perky vegetable.
Makes 8 servings

8 firm ripe tomatoes
8 fresh mushroom caps
4 tablespoons (½ stick) butter or margarine
1 teaspoon seasoned salt
8 pitted ripe olives
8 sprigs mint

1 Trim stem ends from tomatoes. Wash mushrooms.
2 Melt butter or margarine in a medium-size frying pan; add tomatoes and mushrooms, turning in butter to coat well. Sprinkle with seasoned salt; cover.
3 Steam 5 minutes, or just until tomatoes are heated through and skins start to crack.

4 Lift tomatoes onto a serving platter; top each with a mushroom cap, olive and sprig of mint held in place with a wooden pick.

Herbed Lamb Roast
Plan ahead, as meat takes several hours to season in a zippy marinade before roasting.
Roast at 325° for 2½ to 3 hours. Makes 6 servings, with enough for another meal

Buy a leg of young spring lamb, weighing about 7 pounds. Trim off all fat. (Roast will now weigh about 6 pounds.) Place in large shallow pan. Pour HERB MARINADE *(recipe follows)* over; cover. Chill several hours or overnight, turning meat a few times to season evenly. Remove pan with meat from refrigerator about an hour before ready to roast; let stand, turning and basting several times with marinade in pan. Place meat on rack, rounded side up, in roasting pan; pour marinade over. If using a meat thermometer, stick it into the thickest meaty part without touching bone. Do not cover pan. Roast in slow oven (325°), allowing 25 minutes per pound or about 2½ hours for pinky-medium (165° to 170°), and 30 minutes per pound or about 3 hours for well done (180°). Remove to heated

1587

serving platter; slice and serve with GOLDEN GRAVY *(recipe follows).*

HERB MARINADE—Combine ½ cup olive oil or vegetable oil, ¼ cup lemon juice, 1 teaspoon seasoned salt, 1 teaspoon seasoned pepper, 1 teaspoon crumbled leaf marjoram and 1 teaspoon crumbled leaf thyme in jar with tight-fitting cover; shake well to mix. Makes ¾ cup.

GOLDEN GRAVY—Remove rack from roasting pan; tip pan and let fat rise in one corner; pour off all fat into a cup, leaving juices in pan. Return 4 tablespoons fat to pan; blend in 4 tablespoons all-purpose flour; cook, stirring all the time, just until mixture bubbles. Stir in 2 cups water slowly; continue cooking and stirring, scraping baked-on juices from bottom and sides of pan, until gravy thickens and boils 1 minute. Season to taste with salt and pepper. Strain into heated serving bowl. Makes 2 cups.

KNOW THE ART OF CARVING ROAST LEG OF LAMB

It's a meaty cut, and once you know where the bones are, roast is simple to carve into neat generous slices. These illustrated steps show how:

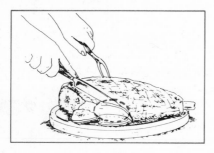

1 Set roast on board before carver with rounded meaty part on far side, shank bone, or small end, at carver's right. Steadying roast with fork, carve a few slices from front to make stand-up base.

2 Turn roast upright on base with meaty rounded part facing up. Starting at shank end,

slice meat, cutting down each time until knife touches leg bone. Continue slicing to bone near fork.

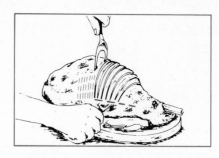

3 Run knife along leg bone to free the slices; lift onto plates. For seconds, make cuts about 1 inch deep into thick front portion (dotted lines at left). Cut around bone to release each small slice.

Stuffed Lamb Roll

This half leg of lamb may look small when boned and stuffed, but it can make two generous meals.

Roast at 325° about 2 hours. Makes enough for 2 meals, 4 servings each

> MINTED BROWN RICE STUFFING *(recipe follows)*
> 1 *five-pound butt end leg of lamb*
> *Seasoned salt*
> SAVORY LAMB GRAVY *(recipe follows)*

1 Mix stuffing and let simmer while boning meat; cool slightly.

2 Lay roast on counter, meaty side down so fat and bony side is up. Trim all fat so bone shows. Using a small very sharp knife and feeling along bone as you go, cut away meat in one piece. Work slowly, pulling away meat to expose bone so you will know where to cut. The bone you cut out will be flat with a round socket. Boning meat may sound difficult, but it's quite simple once you try it.

3 Lay boned meat flat, skin side down, on counter. Mound about 1 cup stuffing in middle. Roll up into a 6- to 7-inch-long roast; tie with string. Sprinkle generously with seasoned salt.

4 Place remaining stuffing in a 6-cup baking dish; cover; bake along with roast during last hour, or until rice is tender.

5 Place roast, skin side up, on rack in roasting pan. Do not add water or cover pan. If using meat thermometer, insert bulb into thickest meaty part (not stuffing).

6 Roast in slow oven (325°), allowing 40 minutes per pound, or about 2 hours for well done. Thermometer should register 180°.

7 Place roast on heated serving platter; cut

One of the loveliest of all lamb recipes, Pimiento-Stuffed Lamb, aromatic of parsley, basil, rosemary.

away string. Slice and serve with SAVORY LAMB GRAVY.

8 Wrap leftover meat and chill for another meal.

SAVORY LAMB GRAVY—Remove the rack from roasting pan. Tip pan and let fat rise in one corner; skim off all fat into a cup, leaving juices in pan. Return 4 tablespoons fat to pan; blend in 4 tablespoons all-purpose flour; cook, stirring all the time, just until mixture bubbles. Stir in 2 cups water slowly; continue cooking and stirring, scraping baked-on juices from bottom and sides of pan, until gravy thickens and boils 1 minute. Season to taste with salt and pepper. Makes about 2 cups.

Minted Brown-Rice Stuffing
Toasted rice plus spice and mint make this refreshingly different dressing for lamb. Makes 4 to 6 servings

1 cup uncooked brown rice
4 tablespoons (½ stick) butter or margarine
1 small onion, chopped (¼ cup)
1 cup chopped celery
3 cups water
1½ teaspoons salt
¼ teaspoon ground cinnamon
¼ teaspoon ground nutmeg
½ cup chopped walnuts
1 tablespoon chopped fresh mint
   OR: ½ teaspoon dried mint flakes

1 Sauté rice in butter or margarine just until lightly toasted in medium-size saucepan; push to one side. Add onion and sauté just until soft.
2 Stir in celery, water, salt, cinnamon and nutmeg; cover. Heat to boiling; simmer 40 minutes, or until liquid is absorbed completely. (Rice will be barely tender.) Fold in walnuts and mint.
Note—If baking separately, place in 6-cup baking dish; cover. Bake in slow oven (325°) 1 hour, or until rice is fluffy and tender.

1590

Pimiento-Stuffed Lamb
Roast at 325° for 2½ hours. Makes 8 servings

1 leg of lamb, weighing about 8 pounds
2 tablespoons olive oil
1 cup fresh bread crumbs
1 cup chopped parsley
1½ teaspoons leaf basil, crumbled
½ teaspoon leaf rosemary, crumbled
1 teaspoon garlic salt
¼ teaspoon seasoned pepper

1 can (4 ounces) pimientos, drained and cut in strips
¼ cup sifted all-purpose flour
1½ cups boiling water

1 Order lamb ahead and ask your meatman to bone it, butterfly fashion. (After boning, roast should weigh about 6½ pounds.)
2 Just before cooking, open lamb out flat, fat side down, on counter top. Brush with 1 tablespoon of the olive oil.
3 Combine bread crumbs, parsley, basil, rosemary, garlic salt and pepper in a small bowl; sprinkle half over lamb; arrange pimientos on top. Roll lamb tightly, jelly-roll fashion; tie securely in several places so meat will keep a neat shape during cooking. Place on a rack in a shallow roasting pan. Insert meat thermometer into thickest part of lamb without touching stuffing or fat.
4 Roast in slow oven (325°) 2 hours. Brush top with remaining 1 tablespoon olive oil.
5 Pat remaining crumb mixture over top of lamb. Continue roasting 30 minutes, or until thermometer registers 175° for medium. (If you prefer lamb well done, increase time 10 to 15 minutes, or until thermometer registers 180°.)
6 Remove lamb to a heated serving platter; keep warm while making gravy.
7 Pour all drippings from roasting pan into a 2-cup measure; let stand a few minutes until fat rises to top, then skim off. Measure 4 tablespoons of the fat and return to pan; blend in flour. Cook, stirring constantly, until bubbly. Stir in boiling water and drippings in cup; continue cooking and stirring until gravy thickens and boils 1 minute. Season with salt and pepper, if needed.
8 Frame roast with watercress and a ruffled green-onion flower, if you wish; slice and serve with gravy.

Lamb in Pastry Crust
(Lamb en Croûte)
Roast at 325° for 1 hour and 45 minutes, then at 425° for 20 minutes. Makes 8 servings

¼ pound chicken livers
3 tablespoons butter or margarine
½ cup chopped green onions
¼ pound mushrooms (or mushroom stems from STUFFED MUSHROOMS), trimmed and diced very fine
1 teaspoon salt
¼ teaspoon pepper
⅛ teaspoon leaf thyme, crumbled
⅛ teaspoon leaf rosemary, crumbled
½ cup fresh bread crumbs (1 slice)

1 boned leg of lamb, weighing about 3½ pounds
Vegetable oil
1 package piecrust mix
1 egg
Water
1 can (about 14 ounces) chicken broth
2 tablespoons cornstarch
STUFFED MUSHROOMS (recipe follows)

1 Sauté chicken livers in butter or margarine in a medium-size skillet until no pink remains. Remove from skillet; place in a medium-size bowl; mash with a fork.

2 Sauté green onions and mushrooms in remaining butter or margarine 3 minutes in same skillet; add to chicken livers. Stir in ½ teaspoon of the salt, ⅛ teaspoon of the pepper, thyme and rosemary. Add bread crumbs to bowl; toss to mix.

3 Unroll lamb; spread out on a flat surface; trim off as much fat as possible. Spread surface of meat evenly with liver-mushroom stuffing; roll up, enclosing stuffing securely. Tie roast crosswise with heavy string at one inch intervals; then tie lengthwise. Insert meat thermometer into thickest part of roast so that bulb end reaches center.

4 Roast in slow oven (325°) 1 hour and 45 minutes, or until meat thermometer registers 170° for rare or 180° for well done. Pour drippings into a cup; reserve. Cool lamb for 30 minutes.

5 Prepare piecrust mix, following label direc-tions, or make pastry from your favorite two-crust recipe. Roll out on a lightly floured pastry cloth or board to a 15x10-inch oval. Remove string from lamb, leaving lamb on rack.

6 Place pastry over lamb; tuck in pastry at base, trimming away excess. Roll out pastry trimmings; cut out decorations with tiny hors d'oeuvres cutters.

7 Beat egg in a cup with 2 teaspoons water; brush entire surface of pastry. Place cutouts on pastry; brush again with egg wash.

8 Bake in hot oven (425°) 20 minutes, or until pastry is golden-brown.

9 While pastry bakes, skim and discard fat from drippings; pour drippings into a medium-size saucepan; stir in chicken broth. Blend cornstarch with a small amount of water until smooth in a cup; pour into saucepan; cook, stirring constantly, until sauce thickens and bubbles 3 minutes.

10 Carefully remove lamb to warm platter. Place STUFFED MUSHROOMS around lamb. Garnish platter with buttered baby carrots and chicory, if you wish.

Stuffed Mushrooms
(with Lamb en Croûte)
Bake at 325° for 20 minutes. Makes 8 servings

16 medium-size mushrooms
 1 package (10 ounces) frozen peas
¼ cup cream for whipping
 2 tablespoons butter or margarine

Lamb in Pastry Crust is filled with a chicken liver pâté, rolled, then wrapped in a wispy-flaky pastry.

1591

2 tablespoons all-purpose flour
½ teaspoon salt
½ teaspoon leaf thyme, crumbled
⅛ teaspoon pepper
2 teaspoons grated onion

1 Remove stems from mushrooms (they can be used for stuffing in LAMB IN PASTRY CRUST or in soup, if you wish). Wipe caps with a damp cloth; place, hollow sides up, in a single layer in a buttered baking dish.
2 Cook peas, following label directions; drain. Place cream in electric-blender container; add cooked peas, a few spoonfuls at a time; whirl at low speed, then at high speed after each addition, until mixture is smooth. Scrape down sides of container often. (If you do not have a blender, press peas through a sieve into a medium-size bowl to purée; stir in cream.)
3 Melt butter or margarine in a medium-size saucepan; stir in flour, salt, thyme and pepper. Cook, stirring constantly, just until bubbly; stir in puréed pea mixture and onion; continue cooking and stirring until mixture thickens and bubbles 1 minute. (It will be very thick.) Place in pastry bag with large star tip; press out into mushroom caps in baking dish. (If you don't have a pastry bag, spoon into caps, mounding mixture.)
4 Bake in slow oven (325°) 20 minutes, or until mushrooms are tender.

Swedish Braised Lamb Shoulder
Makes 8 servings

1 boned and rolled lamb shoulder, weighing about 4 pounds
3 large onions, chopped (3 cups)
1½ cups finely chopped carrots
1 can (10½ ounces) condensed beef bouillon
1½ cups strong black coffee
2 teaspoons salt
½ teaspoon freshly ground pepper
½ cup cream for whipping
2 tablespoons chopped parsley

1 Brown lamb on all sides in a large heavy kettle or Dutch oven. Remove from kettle; reserve. Sauté onion and carrot in pan drippings until soft. Stir in beef bouillon, coffee, salt and pepper. Return meat to kettle; reduce heat; cover.
2 Simmer, turning meat several times, 1½ hours. Add cream and continue cooking 30 minutes longer, or until meat is tender. Remove lamb to heated platter; keep warm.
3 Strain cooking liquid into a medium-size saucepan, pressing vegetables through sieve

1592

with a wooden spoon. Add parsley. Heat slowly until very hot, but do not boil. Serve separately to spoon over meat.

Pot-Roasted Cassoulet of Lamb
Traditional casserole of lamb and beans inspires an inviting pot-roast meal.
Makes 8 servings

1 rolled boned lamb shoulder, weighing about 4 pounds
2 large onions, chopped (2 cups)
2 cloves of garlic, crushed
1 can (10½ ounces) condensed beef broth
1 can (8 ounces) tomato sauce
1 cup chopped fresh mint
  OR: 4 tablespoons dried mint flakes, crumbled
2 teaspoons leaf oregano, crumbled
½ teaspoon ground coriander
¼ teaspoon pepper
  Water
1 package (1 pound) dried large white beans
2 teaspoons salt

1 Brown lamb slowly in a Dutch oven or electric skillet; remove and set aside.
2 Sauté onions and garlic until soft in drippings in Dutch oven; stir in beef broth, tomato sauce, mint, oregano, coriander, pepper and 1 cup water; return meat. Heat to boiling; cover.
3 Simmer, turning meat several times, 2½ hours, or until tender; remove to a cutting board.
4 While lamb cooks, place beans in a large saucepan; add water to cover; heat to boiling; cover. Cook 2 minutes; remove from heat. Let stand 1 hour; stir in salt; cover again. Cook 30 minutes, or until beans are tender.
5 Let broth in Dutch oven stand a few minutes until fat rises to top, then skim off. Strain broth into a bowl, pressing onions through sieve; stir mixture into beans. Spoon onto a heated large deep platter.
6 Carve lamb into ¼-inch-thick slices; arrange over beans.

Roast Lamb Provençal
Roast at 325° for about 2 hours. Makes 16 servings

1 boned lamb shoulder (about 4 pounds)
2 slices whole-wheat bread, trimmed

1 tablespoon milk
4 ounces cooked ham, very finely chopped (¾ cup)
½ cup thinly sliced pimiento-stuffed olives
2 tablespoons very finely chopped onion
1 clove of garlic, minced
¾ teaspoon salt
½ teaspoon leaf basil, crumbled
¼ teaspoon pepper
2 teaspoons olive oil
3 tablespoons cornstarch
  Water
1 envelope instant chicken broth
  OR: 1 teaspoon granulated chicken bouillon

1 Spread lamb shoulder out flat on a cutting board; trim off all inside fat; leave a thin layer of fat on outside of roast.
2 Cut bread into ¼-inch cubes; place in a medium-size bowl; sprinkle with milk; add ham, ¼ cup of the olives, onion and garlic to bowl; toss to mix well. Sprinkle with ¼ teaspoon of the salt, basil and ⅛ teaspoon of the pepper; toss again.
3 Spread stuffing mixture evenly over surface of lamb, pressing firmly. Roll up lamb to enclose stuffing securely. Tie roast crosswise with heavy string at 1-inch intervals, then tie lengthwise. Rub surface with olive oil; sprinkle with remaining salt and pepper; place on a rack in roasting pan. Insert meat thermometer into thickest part of roast so that bulb end reaches center.
4 Roast in slow oven (325°) 2 hours, or until meat thermometer registers 170° for rare or 180° for well done. Remove roast to carving board.
5 Combine cornstarch with small amount of water in a 2-cup measure; blend until smooth. Skim and discard fat from roast drippings. Stir drippings into cornstarch mixture; add water to make 2 cups; pour into a small saucepan; stir in instant chicken broth and remaining olives. Cook, stirring constantly, until sauce thickens and bubbles for 3 minutes.
6 Remove string from lamb roast; cut into thin slices; serve with olive sauce.

Polynesian Lamb
Fruity curry-sparked sauce glazes meat as it cooks.
Makes 6 servings

3 to 4 pounds rolled boned lamb shoulder
2 teaspoons curry powder
1 large onion, chopped (1 cup)
1 clove of garlic, minced
1½ teaspoons salt
1 teaspoon ground allspice
1 cup water

¼ cup lemon juice
1 jar (about 8 ounces) junior prunes
1 jar (about 8 ounces) junior applesauce-and-apricots

1 Rub lamb with curry powder. Brown slowly in heavy kettle or Dutch oven; remove and set aside for Step 3.
2 Sauté onion and garlic until soft in same kettle; stir in salt, allspice, water and lemon juice. Heat to boiling; stir in junior fruits.
3 Return browned meat to kettle; cover. Simmer 2 to 2½ hours, or until tender.
4 Remove to carving board or heated serving platter. Spoon sauce into separate bowl to serve over meat.

PORK AND HAM

FRESH PORK ROASTS TO SUIT YOUR PURSE AND PURPOSE

From regal crown roast to humble pork shoulder, your supermarket offers choices well worth considering from every angle. The pointers below will help you get the most for the money and the occasion.

The New Look:
Modern pork displays show the results of a quiet revolution started several years ago when meat-marketing experts teamed up to produce leaner porkers. For today's shoppers this means bigger value for the money. And dietwise, it means that a serving of pork has far more protein and fewer calories than it had just a few years back.

Shopping Guidelines:
It's easy to spot top quality by looks, so most fresh pork cuts are not stamped with Government grades, as is beef. Signs to go by: Firm, fine-texture lean meat that's a delicate pinkish white, marked with flecks of fat; a snowy-white fat covering; and cut edges of bone that are light pink in color. Checking the fat on the outside is most important, since as it melts during cooking, it adds flavor and juiciness to the meat.

Where to Start Your Buying:
Read your supermarket's newspaper ads to find out which cuts are in good supply and at what prices, then do some armchair thinking before you shop. For example, a center-cut loin

1593

roast—most in demand—will cost more than a loin-end or rib-end roast. But either of these two has the same inviting flavor and is just as easy to fix as a center-cut is, at quite a saving. A boned, trimmed and rolled roast carries a higher price tag because of extra labor costs. But it may actually be thriftier—depending on your circumstances. What you're buying is all meat and no waste, and that means you get more servings from each pound. If you want to go all-out for a party, consider a tenderloin or a crown roast, each deluxe in price but so worth the splurge for special occasions. To see how well you can identify the most popular choices, check the guide. Names may vary across the country, and not all cuts will be available every time you shop, but you'll find a selection big enough to offer you variety.

Let's Come to Terms on Ham:

Here we're talking *fresh ham* only, although the same names apply to the smoked types. It's wise to know the differences between them, for prices vary accordingly. All of us recognize a whole ham, but you'll also find parts marked BUTT HALF or SHANK HALF (each is half of a whole ham) or BUTT PORTION or SHANK PORTION—your clues that slices have been removed from the center of the leg for steaks or a thick roast. Identify the butt half or portion by its slightly rounded end and small round bone just off center. The shank half or portion contains the knucklebone and bony shank or hock. In price, shank half and portion are lowest; butt half and portion, next highest because both contain more meat; and center slices or a roast, highest of all.

Inside Facts on Storage:

Like all meat, fresh pork is perishable, so take care of it properly. If you plan to cook your roast within a day after purchase, no need to unwrap—just chill it. If you want to hold it from two to four days, loosen the store wrapper so air can circulate around the meat, then place it in the coldest part of your refrigerator. For freezer storage, six months is a good time limit. After cooking, cover any leftover meat and chill it promptly.

Center-Cut Loin—The heart of a whole loin. Weighs 3 to 5 pounds, contains part of the tenderloin, ribs and backbone.
Boston Butt—Thrifty square or oblong shoulder

1594

Portrait of three glorious pork roasts (left to right): Crown Roast of Pork Scandia, Tahitian Pork and Barbecued Pork Roll. All are showy but surprisingly simple.

THE CUTS OF PORK AND HAM AND HOW TO COOK THEM

Retail Cuts

Wholesale Cuts

Retail Cuts

2 — **Boneless Loin Roast** — Roast

1 — **Tenderloin** — Frenched and whole — Roast, Braise, Panfry

2 to 5 — **Canadian Style Bacon** — Roast, Broil, Panbroil, Panfry

3 — **Loin Chop**

4 — **Rib Chop**

4 — **Frenched Rib Chop**

2 to 5 — **Butterfly Chop**

— Braise or Panfry —

1-2 — **Sirloin Roast**

3-4 — **Loin Roast** — Center Cut

5 — **Blade Loin Roast**

4 — **Crown Roast**

— Roast —

Fat Back — Lard-Salt Pork

LAB LARD — **Lard** — Shortening

Blade Steaks — Braise, Panfry

Smoked Shoulder Butt — Roast (Bake), Cook in Liquid, Broil, Panbroil, Panfry

Boston Butt

Rolled Boston Butt

— Roast —

HAM

LOIN

SIDE

SPARE RIBS

BOSTON BUTT

PICNIC

JOWL

Jowl Bacon Square — Cook in Liquid, Broil, Panbroil, Panfry

Ham (Butt Half)

Ham (Shank Half) — Roast (Bake), Cook in Liquid

Ham Butt Slice

Center Ham Slice

— Broil, Panbroil, Panfry —

Fresh Ham Roast

Rolled Fresh Ham Roast

— Roast —

Bacon

Salt Pork — Broil, Panbroil, Panfry, Cook in Liquid

Spare Ribs — Roast (Bake), Braise, Cook in Liquid

Fresh Picnic Shoulder — Roast

Smoked Picnic Shoulder — Roast (Bake), Cook in Liquid

Cushion Picnic Shoulder

Rolled Fresh Picnic Shoulder

— Roast —

Fresh Shoulder Hock — Braise, Cook in liquid

Arm Steak — Braise, Panfry

cut, sold bone-in, boneless or boned and rolled. Weighs 4 to 6 pounds.

Crown Roast—Special-order choice, made from rib sections of two loins. Rib-end trims may be ground and stuffed inside.

Sirloin—Meaty roast with part of the tenderloin. Weighing 3 to 4 pounds, it comes from loin end nearest ham section.

Shank Half of Fresh Ham—Lower part of pork leg with shank and leg bone. Not smoked or cured. Weighs 4 to 7 pounds.

Tenderloin—Long, tapering piece of boneless meat, luxury-priced. Weighs about a pound. A carver's dream. Order it ahead.

THE MANY KINDS OF HAM

A big cooked ham can get you off to a head start for many a family and party meal. And where else can you find a more popular meat? Most plentiful in your supermarket are smoked hams—COOK-BEFORE-EATING and FULLY COOKED; fresh hams that look and taste like pork; and ready-to-eat canned boneless hams. Notes here tell about these and others.

Cook-Before-Eating Ham is the familiar regular smoked variety that must be cooked thoroughly. Wrapper directions tell how; or bake in a slow oven (325°), figuring 20 minutes to the pound for a whole ham and 25 minutes for a half ham. If you use a meat thermometer, it should register 160°. You can buy this ham whole—with bone in, partly boned (all removed but the leg bone) or boneless. Some are skinned and trimmed. Weights start at about 8 pounds. This same ham is cut and sold as butt half (chubby rounded shape) and shank half (slightly pointed shape). Often, too, thick center slices are cut from each half and sold for little "roasts" or steaks. Then the remaining butt and shank pieces are labeled PORTIONS or ENDS. Both are excellent buys for a small family or for only one meal.

Fully Cooked Ham means just what it says—no further cooking needed. You can slice it to serve cold, or slide it into the oven just until heated through. It will take about 10 minutes per pound in a slow oven (325°) for a whole ham, 15 minutes for a half ham. Thermometer should register 130°. This ham has very little shrinkage (processing has taken care of that), so even if the price per pound is slightly higher than that for other types, it gives more meaty slices per pound. Like cook-before-eating ham, it comes trimmed, boned, halved and sliced. And you can buy a whole ham weighing as little as 8 pounds.

Boneless Ham might be called party ham; it is a carver's delight. Shaped like a whole ham, an oval or a roll, it can be baked and glazed the same as cook-before-eating ham. For a special buffet party, you might like to ask your meatman to slice this ham on his machine, then tie in its original shape, ready for you to bake and glaze. He will be glad to do this during slow shopping hours.

Canned Ham is boneless, skinless, trimmed and fully cooked. All are cured, but not all are smoked. If you prefer a smoky flavor, check the label. You'll find a variety of sizes to fit any need, with weights ranging from 1 to about 14 pounds. Any canned ham weighing 2 pounds or more is perishable and must be kept in the refrigerator. Most 1-pounders may be stored in the cupboard, but be sure to read the label first. It clearly gives storage directions, plus instructions for heating or baking. Newest in canned hams are "flavored" specialties with a glaze of sugar or honey sparked with mustard and cloves. At Christmas time, fruit-topped novelties are available in some supermarkets.

Country-Style Ham, known best as old-fashioned ham, carries names such as Virginia, Tennessee, Georgia, Kentucky, Smithfield. Although not available everywhere, it is prized by lovers of good ham flavor because of its heavy curing, slow smoking and long drying process. This ham needs no refrigeration before cooking and is usually soaked overnight, then simmered very slowly until tender. Carve it into paper-thin slices to eat with tiny biscuits for a buffet, or slice and pan-fry for breakfast or dinner.

Fresh Ham—simply fresh leg of pork—should be roasted the same as pork loin or ribs to 185° on a meat thermometer. Weights start at about 4 pounds.

Scotch Ham, sometimes called corned ham or sweet-pickle ham, is salt-cured to give it a pinkish tone, but not smoked. Buy it sliced to pan-fry, or roast the same as fresh pork.

Boiled Ham is our familiar "sandwich" favorite and usually comes sliced and packaged, ready for eating.

Prosciutto, or Italian-style Ham makes a big hit as an appetizer meat. Sliced paper-thin, it can be eaten as bought. Its deep ruddy color and zesty flavor contrast pleasantly with fresh fruit, particularly melon.

1597

HOW MUCH HAM SHOULD YOU BUY?

For a Party—Count on a minimum of ¼ pound of boneless cook-before-eating or fully cooked ham for each serving. Or, if buying a whole or half ham with bone in, allow about ½ pound.

For the Family—It's hard to buy too much, as

there are so many ways to turn ham into dividend-best dinners. Slice and pan-fry it for breakfast, or serve it cold with scalloped potatoes or macaroni-and-cheese. Dice and mix it into cream sauce with hard-cooked eggs to serve on toast. Or turn it into ham à la king to spoon over noodles, mashed potatoes or hot corn bread. Chop it for a sandwich spread or to mix with ground beef or veal for a deliciously different meat loaf. And, of course, a ham bone means pea or lentil soup—thick, hearty and wonderfully satisfying!

●

Party Crown Pork Roast
Order this gala roast ahead so your meatman can fix it during slow hours.
Roast at 325° for 2 hours. Makes 8 servings

    1 sixteen-chop crown pork roast
    1 pound ground pork
    1 teaspoon salt
    ½ teaspoon ground cinnamon
    ¼ teaspoon ground cardamom
    ⅛ teaspoon ground allspice
    1 package (8 ounces) ready-mix bread stuffing
    ½ cup water
    1 can (1 pound, 4 ounces) sliced apples, coarsely chopped
    2 tablespoons frozen concentrated orange juice (from a 6-ounce can)
    2 tablespoons honey

1 Place roast, rib ends up, in a large shallow baking pan. (If using a meat thermometer, insert bulb into meaty portion of one chop without touching bone.)
2 Shape ground pork into a large patty in a medium-size frying pan; brown 5 minutes on each side, then break up into chunks. Continue cooking, stirring often, until no pink remains. Stir in salt, cinnamon, cardamom and allspice.
3 Combine bread-stuffing mix and water in a large bowl; stir in pork mixture, chopped apples and any liquid from can. (Stuffing will be crumbly.)
4 Pack into hollow in roast, mounding slightly; cover stuffing with foil to keep it from over-browning.
5 Roast in slow oven (325°) 1 hour; remove foil. Mix concentrated orange juice and honey in a cup; brush part over meat and stuffing. Roast, brushing meat and stuffing every 15 minutes with remaining orange mixture, 1 hour longer, or until meat is tender and richly glazed. (Thermometer should register 170°.)
6 Lift roast carefully onto a carving board or heated platter with two wide spatulas; cut away strings. Garnish roast with thin slices of red apple and sprigs of watercress, if you wish.
7 To carve, start in center of stuffing and cut between ribs into wedges.

●

Crown Roast of Pork Scandia
Roast at 325° for 2 hours. Makes 8 servings

    1 sixteen-chop crown pork roast
    ½ pound ground lean pork
    4 tablespoons (½ stick) butter or margarine
    ½ cup water
    2 cups packaged corn-bread stuffing mix (from an 8-ounce package)
    ½ cup chopped pitted dried prunes
    1 can (6 ounces) frozen concentrate for orange juice
    ½ cup light corn syrup
    2 tablespoons catsup

1 Place roast, rib ends up, on a piece of foil in a shallow roasting pan. (Foil will hold stuffing in roast when it's removed from pan.) Wrap ends of bones with foil to prevent darkening. Insert meat thermometer into roast so bulb reaches center of one chop without touching bone.
2 Roast in slow oven (325°) 1 hour, or until thermometer registers 160°.
3 While roast cooks, shape ground pork into a patty in a large frying pan; brown 5 minutes

Regal Party Crown Roast of Pork wears an apple tiara.

on each side, then break into small chunks. Continue cooking until no pink remains; stir in butter or margarine and water. Pour over stuffing mix and prunes in a large bowl; toss until evenly moist.

4 Blend orange concentrate with corn syrup and catsup in a small saucepan; heat to boiling; simmer 2 minutes.

5 Pack stuffing lightly into hollow in roast, mounding slightly; brush outside of roast and top of stuffing with part of the orange mixture.

6 Continue roasting, brushing several more times with remaining orange mixture, 1 hour, or until thermometer registers 170° and pork is tender and richly glazed.

7 Lift roast carefully onto a heated large serving platter; remove foil from bottom and ends of ribs. Decorate ribs with paper frills; frame roast with small bunches of seedless green grapes, halved orange slices, and watercress, if you wish.

8 Carve roast between ribs into serving-size pieces.

Polynesian Crown Roast

Roast at 325° for 2 hours. Makes 8 servings

    1 sixteen-chop crown pork roast
 1½ cups sliced celery
    1 small onion, chopped (¼ cup)
    4 tablespoons (½ stick) butter or margarine
 ½ pound ground lean pork
 1½ cups cooked rice
 ¼ cup chopped chutney
    2 tablespoons chopped parsley
 1½ teaspoons curry powder
 ¾ teaspoon salt
 ½ teaspoon leaf thyme, crumbled
 ¼ cup sifted all-purpose flour

1 Place roast, rib ends up, on a piece of foil in a shallow roasting pan. (Foil will hold stuffing in roast when it's removed from pan.) Wrap ends of bones with foil to prevent darkening. Insert meat thermometer into roast so bulb reaches center of one chop without touching bone.

2 Roast in slow oven (325°) 1 hour, or until thermometer registers 160°.

3 While roast cooks, sauté celery and onion in butter or margarine until soft in a medium-size frying pan; remove with a slotted spoon and place in a large bowl. Shape ground pork into a patty in same pan; brown 5 minutes on each side, then break into small chunks. Continue cooking until no pink remains; add to onion mixture with rice, chutney, parsley, curry powder, salt and thyme; toss lightly to mix. Pack lightly into hollow in roast, mounding slightly.

4 Continue roasting, 1 hour, or until thermo-meter registers 170° and pork is tender and richly browned.

5 Lift roast carefully onto a heated large serving platter; remove foil from bottom and ends of ribs; keep warm.

6 Pour drippings from pan into a 2-cup measure; let stand a few minutes until fat rises to top, then skim off. Measure ¼ cup fat and return to pan. Add water to drippings to make 2 cups.

7 Blend flour into fat in pan; cook, stirring constantly, until bubbly. Stir in the 2 cups dripping mixture; continue cooking and stirring until gravy thickens and boils 1 minute. Season with salt and pepper, if needed.

8 Carve roast between ribs into serving-size pieces; serve gravy separately to spoon over meat and stuffing.

Peking Pork

Roast at 325° for 2¼ hours. Makes 8 servings

    1 center-cut loin of pork, weighing about 5 pounds
 ½ cup soy sauce
 ½ cup dry sherry
 ¼ cup firmly packed brown sugar
    1 clove of garlic, crushed
    1 teaspoon crushed anise seeds
    1 teaspoon salt
 ½ teaspoon pepper

1 Trim any excess fat from pork; place pork in a large shallow dish.

2 Combine soy sauce, sherry, brown sugar, garlic, anise seeds, salt and pepper in a jar with a tight-fitting lid; shake well to mix; pour over pork. Let stand, turning meat several times, 4 hours to season.

3 Remove pork from dish; set marinade aside. Place pork on spit, following manufacturer's directions. Insert meat thermometer into end of roast to center without touching bone. Set spit in position in oven; start rotisserie.

4 Roast in slow oven (325°) 1 hour, or until thermometer registers 140°. Brush pork with part of the marinade.

5 Continue roasting, brushing often with remaining marinade, 1 hour and 15 minutes, or until thermometer registers 170° and pork is tender and richly glazed.

6 Remove pork from oven; take out spit. Place pork on a heated large serving platter; garnish with preserved kumquats and bouquets of parsley, if you wish. Carve roast between ribs into serving-size pieces.

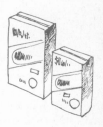

1599

Orange-Glazed Pork

Tangy sauce seasons the roast as it glazes sparkly brown.
Roast at 325° about 2 hours. Makes 4 servings

1 four-pound loin of pork
1 small onion, grated
1 tablespoon butter or margarine
2 tablespoons brown sugar
1½ teaspoons cornstarch
½ teaspoon ground ginger
1 cup orange juice
1 tablespoon bottled steak sauce

1 Place pork, fat side up, on rack in a roasting pan. If using a meat thermometer, insert bulb into center of meat without touching bone.
2 Roast in slow oven (325°) 1 hour. While pork roasts, sauté onion in butter or margarine until soft in a small saucepan; stir in remaining ingredients. Cook, stirring constantly, until thick.
3 Brush part over meat. Continue roasting, brushing meat every 15 minutes, 1 hour longer, or until richly glazed and thermometer registers 170°. Carve meat into chops.

Savory Pork Roast

One four-pound loin of pork gives you two treats: a small roast plus chops for another meal.
Roast at 325° about 1½ hours. Makes 2 meals, 2 servings each

1 four-pound loin of pork (about 8 chops)
2 tablespoons all-purpose flour
2 teaspoons salt
½ teaspoon leaf sage, crumbled
½ teaspoon paprika
¼ teaspoon pepper

1 Cut 4 chops from loin and save to cook another day.
2 Mix flour with seasonings; rub over roast to coat well. If using a meat thermometer, insert bulb into center of roast without touching bone.
3 Roast in slow oven (325°) about 1½ hours, or until thermometer registers 170°.
Note—For 4 servings, leave roast whole and use the same amounts of flour and seasonings as given above. Roast in slow oven (325°) about 2 hours, or until thermometer registers 170°.

1600

Fruit-Stuffed Pork Roast

Watch for a special on pork loin, then treat the family to this "big splurge."
Bake at 325° about 2½ hours. Makes 6 to 8 servings

1 five-pound loin of pork (about 12 chops)
1 large onion, chopped (1 cup)
4 tablespoons (½ stick) butter or margarine
¾ cup water
1 can (6 ounces) frozen concentrated orange juice
1 package (8 ounces) ready-mix bread stuffing (4 cups)
½ cup chopped dried prunes
¼ cup firmly packed brown sugar
½ teaspoon dry mustard
1 tablespoon bottled savory sauce

1 Place roast on a cutting board with ends of ribs up and meat side toward you. Make slits between chops about 2 inches deep for pockets for stuffing.
2 Sauté onion in butter or margarine until soft in a medium-size saucepan; stir in water and ¼ cup concentrated orange juice. (Set remaining orange juice aside for Step 6.) Heat just to boiling; remove from heat; stir in bread stuffing and prunes until well moistened.
3 Stuff about ½ cup into each pocket of roast, packing it in well and mounding any extra stuffing over pocket.
4 Place roast, stuffing side up, on rack in a shallow roasting pan. If using a meat thermometer, insert bulb into center of meat without touching bone. Cover pan loosely with foil.
5 Roast in slow oven (325°) 1½ hours, or until thermometer registers 165°; remove foil.
6 Combine remaining concentrated orange juice, brown sugar, mustard and savory sauce in a small saucepan; heat slowly, stirring once or twice, just until sugar dissolves.
7 Brush part over meat (not stuffing). Continue roasting, basting every 15 minutes with more orange-sugar mixture, about 1 hour longer, or until meat is very tender and thermometer registers 170°.
8 Remove roast to heated serving platter; carve into chops, each with its own stuffing.

Roast Pork Bavarian

Spicy-tart stuffing of sauerkraut, apple and raisin spills out of each succulent chop.
Roast at 325° about 3 hours. Makes enough for 2 meals, 6 servings each

1 six-pound loin of pork (about 14 chops)
1 can (about 1 pound) sauerkraut, drained and chopped
2 cups slightly dry bread cubes (4 slices)
1 medium-size apple, diced
½ cup seedless raisins
1 small onion, minced
½ teaspoon salt
½ teaspoon poultry seasoning

Orange-Glazed Pork takes the choicest cut of loin, roast it every-so-slowly and jewel it with glaze.

¼ teaspoon caraway seeds
⅛ teaspoon pepper
  BROWN PORK GRAVY (recipe follows)

1 Place meat on board with rib ends up and meat side toward you. Slit each chop clear through to bone to make a pocket for stuffing.
2 Mix remaining ingredients, except gravy, in large bowl; stuff about ½ cup into each pocket, packing in well. Tie roast with string.

3 Place, fat side up, on rack in shallow roasting pan. If using meat thermometer, insert bulb into center of meat without touching bone. Do not add water or cover pan.
4 Roast in slow oven (325°), allowing 30 to 35 minutes per pound, or about 3 hours. Thermometer should register 170°.
5 Place roast on heated serving platter; cut away string. Carve into chops—each will have its own stuffing. Serve with BROWN PORK GRAVY.

6 Wrap leftover meat with stuffing and chill for another meal.

BROWN PORK GRAVY—Remove rack from roasting pan. Tip pan and let fat rise in one corner; skim off all fat into a cup, leaving juices in pan. Return 4 tablespoons fat to pan; blend in 4 tablespoons all-purpose flour; cook, stirring all the time, just until mixture bubbles. Stir in 2 cups water slowly; continue cooking and stirring, scraping baked-on juices from bottom and sides of pan, until gravy thickens and boils 1 minute. Season to taste with salt and pepper; stir in a few drops of gravy coloring to darken, if you wish. Makes 2 cups.

Beer-Braised Loin of Pork

Tender, juicy pork is the flavorful result of the long, slow cooking in the dark beer. This oven-braising is a nice time-saver, no watching necessary.

Braise at 350° for 2 hours. Makes 8 servings

1 pork loin roast, about 5 pounds
3 large onions, chopped (3 cups)
1 pound carrots, peeled and diced
1 bottle or can (12 ounces) dark beer
2 teaspoons salt
¼ teaspoon pepper
1 bay leaf
5 whole cloves

1 Brown pork loin well on all sides in a kettle or Dutch oven; remove from pan. (Or brown in a large heavy roasting pan on surface burners.)
2 Sauté onions and carrots until soft in pork drippings. Stir in beer, salt, pepper, bay leaf and whole cloves. Return pork to kettle and cover. (If using roasting pan, cover tightly with aluminum foil.)
3 Braise in moderate oven (350°) 2 hours, or until pork is tender when pierced with a two-tined fork. Place pork on platter and keep warm.
4 Pour cooking liquid from kettle into a large bowl. Skim off fat; remove bay leaf. Place liquid and solids in container of electric blender and whirl at low speed until smooth (or press through sieve). Pour sauce into saucepan. Heat to boiling, stirring often. Stir in a little gravy coloring, if you wish. Generously spoon the sauce over the pork after it has been sliced.

1602

Tarragon Pork Roast
Roast at 325° for 2 hours. Makes 6 servings

1 rolled boned center-cut loin of pork, weighing about 3 pounds
1 teaspoon salt
½ teaspoon pepper

6 sprigs fresh tarragon
OR: 1 teaspoon leaf tarragon, crumbled
4 tablespoons (½ stick) butter or margarine
1¼ cups dry white wine
2 tablespoons all-purpose flour

1 Rub pork with salt and pepper; place on a rack in a shallow roasting pan. Lay sprigs of tarragon over meat. (If using dried tarragon, crumble it evenly over meat.) Insert meat thermometer into roast so bulb reaches center.
2 Melt butter or margarine in a small saucepan; stir in 1 cup of the wine; pour part over roast.
3 Roast in slow oven (325°), spooning remaining wine mixture over meat several times, 2 hours, or until thermometer registers 170°. Remove roast to a heated serving platter; keep warm.
4 Let liquid in roasting pan stand a few minutes until fat rises to top, then skim off; reheat liquid to boiling. (There should be about 1 cupful, but, if needed, add enough water or wine to measure this amount.)
5 Blend flour with remaining ¼ cup wine until smooth in a cup; stir into boiling liquid. Cook, stirring constantly, until gravy thickens and boils 1 minute.
6 Slice roast ¼ inch thick, removing strings as you carve; serve gravy separately to spoon over meat.

Scandinavian Pork Pot
Makes 4 servings

1 rib-end pork loin, about 7 ribs, backbone cracked (about 3 pounds)
2 tablespoons vegetable oil
2 teaspoons salt
½ teaspoon ground ginger
¼ teaspoon pepper
¼ teaspoon dry mustard
1 large orange
1 lemon
Water
2 tablespoons dark corn syrup
1 pound small white onions, peeled
1 cup dried apricots
1 cup pitted prunes
1 tablespoon cornstarch

1 Trim excess fat from pork; brown on all sides in vegetable oil in a kettle or Dutch oven. Sprinkle with salt, ginger, pepper and mustard.
2 Meanwhile, remove the thin bright-colored peel from the orange and lemon with a sharp knife; reserve. Squeeze juice from orange and

lemon into a 1-cup measure; add water to make 1 cup liquid. Stir into kettle with corn syrup and rinds. Heat to boiling; reduce heat; cover. Simmer 1½ hours.

3 Add onions, apricots and prunes; simmer 1 hour longer, or until pork is tender. Place pork on a heated serving platter. Remove onions, apricots and prunes from kettle with a slotted spoon and arrange on meat platter. Discard orange and lemon peels. Skim fat from cooking liquid in kettle.

4 To make gravy: Combine cornstarch with small amount of water in a cup; stir into cooking liquid in kettle; cook, stirring constantly, until sauce thickens and bubbles 3 minutes. Serve with pork.

Canyon Pork Roast

Roast at 325° for 2½ hours. Makes 8 servings

1 rib-end loin of pork, weighing about 5 pounds
8 walnut halves
16 dried apricot halves
1 can (about 5 ounces) apricot nectar
¼ cup honey
2 tablespoons butter or margarine
2 tablespoons lemon juice

1 Trim any excess fat from pork. Place pork on a cutting board with rib ends down. Make a cut lengthwise through middle of meat, cutting down to rib bones.

2 Stuff each walnut half, sandwich style, between apricot halves; push deep into cut in meat. Tie roast in 5 or 6 places with heavy cord to hold in stuffing.

3 Place roast in a baking pan, 13x9x2. (Ribs form their own rack.) Do not cover pan or add any water. Insert meat thermometer into roast so bulb reaches center without touching either bone or stuffing.

4 Roast in slow oven (325°) 1 hour, or until thermometer registers 140°.

5 Combine apricot nectar, honey, butter or margarine and lemon juice in a small saucepan; heat to boiling. Brush part over pork.

6 Continue roasting, brushing meat with remaining apricot mixture every 15 minutes, 1½ hours, or until thermometer registers 170° and pork is tender and richly glazed.

7 Remove to a heated serving platter; cut away strings. Garnish platter with watercress and more dried apricots, if you wish. Carve roast between ribs into serving-size pieces.

Tenderloin Pinwheels

Bake at 325° for 1½ hours. Makes 6 servings

2 pork tenderloins, weighing about 10 ounces each
½ pound fresh mushrooms
½ cup (1 stick) butter or margarine
1 package (10 ounces) frozen peas
1 package (about 4 ounces) sliced boiled ham, cut in very small pieces
2 cups fine fresh bread crumbs (4 slices)
2 eggs
1 teaspoon salt
¼ teaspoon pepper
1 can (10½ ounces) condensed beef broth

1 Split one of the tenderloins, cutting not quite to opposite side; open out flat, butterfly style. Starting at center, split one half almost to outer edge; open out. Starting at center again, repeat on other side. You now have a flat piece of meat, about 12x8. Prepare other tenderloin the same way.

2 Trim mushrooms and chop very fine; sauté in 4 tablespoons of the butter or margarine until soft in a medium-size frying pan. Spread half evenly over each tenderloin.

3 Cook peas, following label directions; drain. Mash coarsely with a fork in a large bowl; add ham, bread crumbs, eggs, salt and pepper; toss lightly to mix.

4 Spread over mushroom layer on meat. Starting at thinnest end of each tenderloin, roll up, jelly-roll fashion. Tie rolls at 1-inch intervals with string. Set side by side on a rack in a baking pan, 13x9x2.

5 Cook beef broth rapidly in a small saucepan 10 minutes, or until it measures about ¾ cup; stir in remaining 4 tablespoons butter or margarine until melted. Brush part over pork rolls.

6 Bake in slow oven (325°), brushing every 15 minutes with broth mixture, 1½ hours, or until pork is tender and richly glazed. Remove to a heated large serving platter; cut away strings. Slice each roll into thirds.

Barbecued Pork Roll

Roast at 325° for 2½ hours. Makes 12 servings

1 rolled boned center-cut loin of pork, weighing about 6 pounds
1 cup chili sauce
1 large onion, diced (1 cup)
¾ cup maple-blended syrup
1 teaspoon mixed salad herbs
1 teaspoon pumpkin-pie spice

1603

1 Place pork on a rack in a shallow roasting pan. Insert meat thermometer into roast so bulb reaches center.

2 Roast in slow oven (325°) 1½ hours.

3 Combine chili sauce, onion, syrup, salad herbs and pumpkin-pie spice in a small saucepan; heat to boiling. Spoon part over roast to coat generously.

4 Continue roasting, spooning more sauce over meat every 15 minutes, 1 hour, or until thermometer registers 170°. Remove roast to a heated serving platter. Garnish with baked tomato cups stuffed with buttered green beans, and chicory or curly endive, if you wish.

5 Let sauce in pan stand until fat rises to top, then skim off. Reheat sauce to boiling; spoon into a small bowl.

6 Slice roast ¼ inch thick, removing strings as you carve; serve sauce separately to spoon over meat.

●

Tahitian Pork

Roast at 325° for 4 hours. Makes 6 servings, plus enough for one bonus dish

1 butt half fresh ham, weighing about 6 pounds
1 can (6 ounces) pineapple juice
¼ cup lime juice
½ cup firmly packed brown sugar
½ teaspoon whole cloves
2 three-inch pieces stick cinnamon
  Lime slices, halved

1 Trim skin and any excess fat from pork. Place roast on a rack in a shallow baking pan. Insert meat thermometer into roast so bulb reaches thickest part without touching bone.

2 Roast in slow oven (325°) 3½ hours, or until thermometer registers 180°

3 While pork roasts, combine pineapple and lime juices, brown sugar, cloves and cinnamon in a small saucepan; heat to boiling. Simmer 5 minutes. Brush part over roast.

4 Continue roasting, brushing every 10 minutes with remaining pineapple mixture, 30 minutes, or until thermometer registers 185° and pork is tender and richly glazed.

5 Remove to a heated serving platter. Make two cuts lengthwise across top of roast; tuck halved lime slices into cuts; brush with any remaining pineapple mixture. Garnish platter with parsley.

6 Carve roast into ¼-inch-thick slices.

1604

●

Kriss Kringle Stuffed Fresh Ham

Order meat ahead so your meatman can bone it during his slower hours. Homemade biscuits and corn bread make the unusual stuffing.

Roast at 325° about 5 hours. Makes 8 servings, plus enough for another meal

1 whole fresh ham, weighing about 10 pounds
1 cup diced celery
1 medium-size onion, chopped (½ cup)
4 tablespoons (½ stick) butter or margarine
3 cups crumbled slightly dry corn bread
2 cups crumbled slightly dry baking-powder biscuits
¼ cup diced pimiento
1 teaspoon salt
¼ teaspoon leaf thyme, crumbled
1 egg, slightly beaten
1 jar (12 ounces) peach jam
1 tablespoon lemon juice
1 teaspoon prepared mustard
  PETAL-PINK ONION ROSE (directions follow)

1 Ask your meatman to trim skin from ham, then remove leg bone to make a pocket for stuffing. Lightly score fat into diamonds or squares.

2 Sauté celery and onion in butter or margarine until soft in a medium-size frying pan; combine with crumbled corn bread and biscuits, pimiento, salt, thyme and egg in a medium-size bowl; toss until evenly moist. Stuff into pocket in ham; lace opening together with poultry pins or skewers and string.

3 Place ham, fat side up, on a rack in a shallow baking pan; do not add water or cover pan. If using a meat thermometer, insert into thickest part of ham without touching the stuffing.

4 Roast in slow oven (325°) 3½ hours.

5 While meat cooks, combine peach jam, lemon juice and mustard in a small saucepan; heat, stirring constantly, to boiling; brush half over ham.

6 Continue roasting, brushing two or three more times with remaining peach mixture, 1½ hours, or until richly glazed and thermometer registers 185°.

7 Remove to a heated serving platter; let stand 15 to 20 minutes for easier slicing. Garnish platter with a PETAL-PINK ONION ROSE and watercress, if you wish. Carve meat into ¼-inch-thick slices.

PETAL-PINK ONION ROSE—Peel a medium-size Bermuda onion and trim ends. Using a sharp-tip thin-blade knife, cut scallops all around onion about 1 inch up from bottom, cutting just through the first layer. Slit layer from top of onion to scallop line and peel off upper section. Cut a second layer of scallops about ½ inch higher than first, centering each scallop between those on bottom row; peel off section. Continue the same way to top of onion. Place in a bowl of water tinted with red food coloring; let stand several hours, or until edges of onion turn pink. Drain well.

Indonesian Pork Roast

Five ingredients make its exotic sauce that doubles as a baste for the dividend dish.
Makes enough for 2 meals, 4 servings each

    1 fresh pork shoulder butt (5 to 6 pounds)
    1 clove of garlic, minced
    1 chicken-bouillon cube
    ¼ cup sugar
    1 cup water
    ½ cup soy sauce

1 Brown pork in its own fat in large heavy kettle or Dutch oven.
2 Combine remaining ingredients in 2-cup measure; pour over meat; cover.
3 Simmer, turning meat 2 or 3 times, 2 to 2½ hours, or until very tender.
4 Remove meat to heated platter; slice and serve with plain or curried rice and applesauce or bottled chutney.

Golden Glazed Pork

Simmer meat first, then brush with a mellow molasses sauce and bake until sparkly.
Bake at 325° for 45 minutes. Makes 6 servings

    1 smoked boneless pork shoulder butt, weighing about 2½ pounds
    ¼ cup sugar
    ¼ cup molasses
    ¼ teaspoon ground cinnamon
    ⅛ teaspoon ground cloves
    ⅛ teaspoon ground ginger

1 Peel covering from pork shoulder butt. Simmer meat, covered, in water to cover in a kettle 1½ hours, or until tender; drain. Place in a shallow baking pan.
2 Blend sugar with molasses and spices in a small bowl; brush half over meat.
3 Bake in slow oven (325°) 20 minutes; brush with remaining molasses mixture. Bake 25 minutes longer, or until richly glazed. Carve in ¼-inch-thick slices.

Peter Piper Pork

It's a cousin to sauerbraten—and equally good eating.
Bake at 325° about 4 hours. Makes enough for 2 meals, 4 servings each

    1 fresh pork picnic shoulder (about 5 pounds)
    2 cups white vinegar
    2 tablespoons salt
    2 tablespoons sugar
    8 peppercorns
    1 teaspoon celery seeds
    2 bay leaves
    1 clove of garlic, halved
    1 small onion, sliced
    10 to 12 whole cloves

1 Remove thick skin and trim fat layer, if needed, from pork with sharp knife; place pork in a large glass bowl.
2 Combine remaining ingredients, except whole cloves, in 4-cup measure; pour over meat. Cover; chill, turning several times to marinate all sides, 24 hours.
3 When ready to cook, pat meat dry; brown in large heavy kettle or Dutch oven; remove from heat. (If using a meat thermometer, insert in roast so bulb reaches meaty center.) Pour 1 cup marinade over; cover.
4 Roast in slow oven (325°) about 3½ hours, or until very tender. (Meat thermometer should register 185°.)
5 Score fat layer; stud with whole cloves; roast, uncovered, basting often with marinade, 30 minutes longer, or until delicately browned. Remove to heated platter; slice and serve with country-fried potatoes and buttered Brussels sprouts.

Appletime Pork Roast

Pork and apples are hard to beat. This roast stars both the tart fruit and sweet cider.
Bake at 325° about 3½ hours. Makes enough for 2 meals, 4 servings each

    1 fresh pork shoulder butt (about 5 pounds)
    1 teaspoon pumpkin-pie spice
    1 cup apple cider
    2 tart cooking apples, cored and sliced
    2 tablespoons brown sugar
    2 tablespoons all-purpose flour
    2 tablespoons water

1 Brown pork in its own fat in large heavy kettle or Dutch oven; remove from heat. (If using a meat thermometer, insert in roast so bulb reaches meaty center.) Sprinkle meat with pumpkin-pie spice; pour cider over; cover.
2 Bake in slow oven (325°) 3 hours, or until very tender. (Thermometer should register 185°.)

1605

3 Remove meat from kettle. Drain liquid into a 4-cup measure; let stand about a minute, or until fat rises to top; skim off fat. Arrange sliced apples in bottom of kettle; place meat on top; stir brown sugar into drained liquid; pour over meat.

4 Bake, uncovered, basting often with liquid in kettle, 30 minutes longer, or until lightly browned. Remove pork to heated platter; keep hot while making gravy.

5 Smooth flour and water to a paste in cup; slowly stir into hot liquid in kettle. Cook, stirring constantly and scraping baked-on juices from bottom and sides of kettle, until gravy thickens and boils 1 minute. Season with salt and pepper, if needed.

6 Slice meat; serve with gravy to spoon over, and baked potatoes, if you wish.

Caraway Pork

This thrifty meat owes its inviting flavor to these pungent seeds.
Makes 6 servings

4 to 5 pounds fresh pork shoulder butt
2 teaspoons salt
1 teaspoon caraway seeds
¼ teaspoon pepper
1 large clove of garlic, peeled
½ cup water
2 large onions, peeled and cut in thick slices

1 Brown pork slowly in its own fat in heavy kettle or Dutch oven; drain off all fat.

2 Sprinkle salt, caraway seeds and pepper over; add garlic and water; cover.

3 Simmer 2½ hours, or until almost tender. Place onion slices around meat; simmer 30 minutes longer, or until meat is very tender.

4 Remove to carving board or heated serving platter; discard garlic. Spoon onions around meat.

1606

Ginger Glazed Pork Roast

Use this recipe for winter cooking, too, as it works perfectly on a range rotisserie.
Makes 6 servings

1 smoked pork shoulder butt (about 5 pounds)
½ cup apricot jam
¼ cup orange juice
1 teaspoon ground ginger

1 Cut off thick skin from pork shoulder. If fat layer is thick, trim off about half, then score remaining fat in diamonds or squares.

2 Place pork on spit, following manufacturer's directions. (If using a meat thermometer, insert bulb in one end of meat without touching bone.) Set spit in position over hot coals; start rotisserie. (You'll need a fire bed big enough to last about 2 hours.)

3 Roast pork, following manufacturer's directions, about 1½ hours. (Thermometer should register 160°.)

4 Combine jam, orange juice and ginger in small saucepan; heat slowly on side of grill, then brush pork all over as it turns.

5 Continue to grill, brushing often with sauce, 30 minutes longer, or until pork is tender and richly glazed. (Thermometer should register 170°.)

6 Remove meat to cutting board; slice thin.

Jamaican Pork

Makes 6 servings, plus enough for one bonus dish

1 fresh pork shoulder, weighing about 5 pounds
2 teaspoons salt
½ teaspoon pepper
2 tablespoons vegetable oil
3 large onions, chopped (3 cups)
2 cups water
¼ cup cider vinegar
2 tablespoons honey
½ cup sliced pitted ripe olives
½ cup seedless raisins
2 tablespoons capers
⅓ cup flour

1 Trim skin and any excess fat from pork. Sprinkle salt and pepper over meat. Brown slowly in vegetable oil in a heavy kettle or Dutch oven; remove and set aside. Pour all drippings from kettle, then measure 2 tablespoonfuls and return to kettle.

2 Stir onions into drippings; sauté until soft. Stir in water, vinegar, honey, olives, raisins and capers; heat to boiling. Place pork in sauce; cover. Simmer, turning several times, 2½ hours, or until pork is tender.

3 Remove to a heated serving platter; keep warm. Let liquid in kettle stand until fat rises to top, then skim off; reheat liquid to boiling.

4 Blend flour with about 3 tablespoons water to a paste in a cup; stir into boiling liquid. Cook, stirring constantly, until sauce thickens and boils 1 minute.

5 Carve pork into ¼-inch-thick slices; serve sauce separately to spoon over meat.

Onion-Stuffed Pork Roast

Onion stuffing and a savory crisp cereal topping make everyday pork a feast.

Bake at 325° for 4 hours. Makes 6 servings, plus enough for a second meal

- 1 fresh pork shoulder butt (about 5 pounds)
- 1 large onion, peeled and sliced
- ½ teaspoon leaf marjoram, crumbled
- 2 tablespoons butter or margarine
- 2 tablespoons prepared mustard
- 1 cup coarsely crushed bite-size toasted corn cereal
- 2 tablespoons brown sugar
- 1 teaspoon ground cinnamon
- ¼ cup honey
- ¼ cup hot water

1 Ask your meatman to remove the bone from pork shoulder to make a pocket. (Cook bone in pan with roast, if you wish, for extra flavor for drippings.) Score fat on meat into deep 1-inch squares.

2 Sauté onion with marjoram in butter or margarine just until soft in a small frying pan; stuff into pocket in meat. Tie with string to close opening.

3 Spread mustard over top and sides of roast. Place, fat side up, on a rack in a shallow pan; do not cover or add water. If using a meat thermometer, insert bulb into center of meat.

4 Roast in slow oven (325°) 3½ hours, or until thermometer registers 175°. While meat cooks, mix crushed cereal, brown sugar, cinnamon, honey and hot water in a small bowl. Remove roast from oven and cut away string; spread cereal mixture over top, poking it into cuts in fat with a fork.

5 Roast meat 30 minutes longer, or until top is crispy-brown and thermometer registers 185°.

6 Place meat on a cutting board; keep hot while making PAN GRAVY (recipe follows). Carve in about ¼-inch-thick slices.

PAN GRAVY—Remove rack from roasting pan. Tip pan and pour off all fat, leaving drippings in pan. Return 2 tablespoons fat to pan. Blend in 2 tablespoons all-purpose flour; cook, stirring all the time, just until mixture bubbles. Stir in 2 cups water; continue cooking and stirring, scraping baked-on juices from bottom and sides of pan, until gravy thickens and boils 1 minute. Season to taste with salt and pepper. Makes 2 cups.

Harvest Stuffed Pork

Succulent shoulder stuffed with golden corn and herbs oven-braises with no watching.

Bake at 325° about 6 hours. Makes enough for 2 meals, 6 servings each

Onion-Stuffed Pork Roast with crunchy-spicy topping.

Harvest Stuffed Pork is filled with corn and crumbs.

1 *whole boned fresh pork shoulder (about 6 pounds)*
2 *eggs*
4 *cups coarse bread crumbs (8 slices)*
1 *can (12 or 16 ounces) whole-kernel corn, drained*
1 *small onion, chopped (¼ cup)*
2 *teaspoons salt*
½ *teaspoon pepper*
½ *teaspoon ground sage*
½ *cup water*
4 *tablespoons all-purpose flour*
1 *jar (15 ounces) spiced apple rings*
  OVEN GLAZED ONIONS *(recipe follows)*

1 Trim skin layer from pork with sharp knife.
2 Beat eggs in medium-size bowl; stir in bread crumbs, corn, onion, salt, pepper and sage.
3 Stuff cavity in meat with mixture, packing in well to fill and give meat a rounded shape. Tie with string at 1-inch intervals.
4 Brown, fat side first, in large roasting pan; remove from heat. (If using a meat thermometer, insert in roast so bulb reaches meaty center.) Pour water over; cover with lid of roasting pan or heavy foil, fastening around edges of pan to seal.
5 Bake in slow oven (325°) 5½ hours, or just until meat is tender. Remove pork from pan; strain liquid into a 4-cup measure. (Save for Step 6.) Return meat to pan; bake, uncovered, 30 minutes longer, or until richly browned. (Thermometer should register 185°.) Remove pork to heated platter; keep hot.
6 Skim off fat from strained liquid; return 4 tablespoons fat to pan; blend in flour; cook over low heat, stirring constantly, until richly browned. Add water to liquid, if needed, to make 4 cups; stir into browned flour mixture. Cook, stirring constantly and scraping baked-on juices from bottom and sides of pan, until gravy thickens slightly and boils 1 minute. Season with salt and pepper, if needed.
7 Garnish pork platter with spiced apple rings and OVEN-GLAZED ONIONS; serve with gravy to spoon over.
8 Wrap any leftover meat; chill meat and leftover gravy for another meal.

1608

Oven-Glazed Onions

Easy as can be to fix and bake along with pork. Bake at 325° for 30 minutes. Makes 6 servings

6 *large onions, peeled*
4 *tablespoons (½ stick) butter or margarine*
4 *tablespoons brown sugar*
2 *tablespoons water*
½ *teaspoon salt*

1 Parboil onions in boiling salted water in large saucepan 15 to 20 minutes, or until almost tender; drain.
2 Melt butter or margarine in 6-cup shallow baking dish in oven; stir in brown sugar, water and salt. Roll each onion in mixture and arrange in single layer in dish; cover.
3 Bake in slow oven (325°), turning onions 2 or 3 times, 30 minutes, or until tender and golden.

Herbed Stuffed Pork

Roast at 325° for 3 hours. Makes 6 servings, plus enough for one bonus dish

1 *fresh pork shoulder, weighing about 5 pounds, boned*
2 *tablespoons chopped onion*
2 *tablespoons chopped celery*
2 *tablespoons butter or margarine*
2 *cups fresh bread crumbs (4 slices)*
½ *teaspoon salt*
½ *teaspoon leaf rosemary, crumbled*
¼ *teaspoon leaf thyme, crumbled*
¼ *cup finely chopped parsley*
¼ *cup flour*

1 Trim skin and any excess fat from pork.
2 Sauté onion and celery in butter or margarine until soft in a small saucepan. Combine bread crumbs, salt, rosemary, thyme and parsley in a medium-size bowl; pour onion mixture over top; toss until evenly moist.
3 Stuff mixture into pocket in pork, packing in well to give meat a rounded shape. Tie roast in several places to hold in stuffing. Place pork, fat side up, on a rack in a shallow roasting pan. Do not add water or cover pan. Insert meat thermometer into roast so bulb reaches thickest part without touching stuffing.
4 Roast in slow oven (325°) 3 hours, or until thermometer registers 185° and pork is tender. Remove roast to a heated large serving platter; keep warm.
5 Pour all drippings from pan into a 2-cup measure; let stand a few minutes until fat rises to top, then skim off. Measure ¼ cup and return to pan. Add water to drippings to make 2 cups.
6 Blend flour into fat in pan; cook, stirring constantly, until bubbly. Stir in the 2 cups drippings mixture; continue cooking and stirring until gravy thickens and boils 1 minute.
7 Slice roast ¼ inch thick; serve gravy separately to spoon over meat.

Golden-Glaze Baked Ham
Count on a minimum of ¼ pound for each serving of boneless ham, and ½ pound for the bone-in type. This is a good rule of thumb to follow for a party, but for family eating you'll want to plan to have enough left for a dividend dish. Bake ham according to label directions. Or place meat, fat side up, on rack in shallow roasting pan. Do not add water or cover. If fat top is not covered with skin, leave plain or score into 1-inch squares or diamonds. If with skin, bake and then remove skin, scoring fat, if you wish, just before starting to glaze top. If using a meat thermometer, insert into thickest part of meat without touching bone; bake or heat, following the accompanying HAM BAKING TIMETABLE. One hour before ham is done, brush with your favorite glaze or the GOLDEN GLAZE on our pictured ham (recipe follows). Continue baking, glazing every 10 to 15 minutes, or until top is richly golden.

Golden Glaze
Blend 1 cup light molasses and ½ cup prepared mustard in small bowl. Brush on ham for final hour's baking. Makes enough to glaze a 10- to 15-pound ham.

ROASTS, JUICY AND TENDER

HAM BAKING TIMETABLE

Oven temperature: **325°**

Kind of Ham	Minutes per Pound		
	Boneless	Bone-in	Thermometer
Cook-before-eating			
Whole	20 to 25	20	160°
Half	30 to 35	25 to 30	160°
Steak	25 to 30		
Picnic (whole)	30 to 35	25 to 30	170°
Fully cooked			
Whole	10 to 20	15 to 20	130°
Half	20 to 25	20	130°
Steak	20 to 25		
Picnic (whole)	15 to 25	15 to 25	130°
Rolled			
2 to 6 pounds		30 to 40	130°
6 or more pounds		15 to 20	130°
Canned			
Follow label directions. Or:			
Large		15 to 20	130°
Small		20 to 25	130°

Orange Blossom Ham Platter

Boneless ham is a beauty with its golden glaze and garnish—and a cinch to slice.
Bake at 325° for 2 hours. Makes 8 servings plus enough for one bonus meal

- 6 pounds boned rolled ready-to-eat ham
  Orange slices, halved
- 1 can (6 ounces) frozen concentrate for pine-apple-orange juice, thawed
- ¾ cup honey

1 Peel wrapping, if any, from ham; place ham on a rack in a large shallow baking pan. (Do not add water or cover pan.)
2 Bake in slow oven (325°) 1½ hours; remove from oven.
3 Using a sharp thin-blade knife, make parallel cuts, ½ inch deep and ¼ inch apart, in top of ham. Insert half an orange slice in each cut, alternating from side to side. (To notch slices, cut away even sections around rind with a round truffle cutter.)
4 Blend pineapple-orange juice concentrate and honey in a small bowl; brush part over ham and oranges.
5 Continue baking, brushing several times with remaining honey mixture, 30 minutes, or until richly glazed. Remove to a heated large serving platter. Carve ham into ¼-inch-thick slices.

Orange Blossom Ham Platter, shown dressed for a special dinner party. The garnish is far easier than it looks. Slice oranges, quarter and fasten to ham with cloves.

GAY TRIMS FOR HAM

Tips for Glazing and Garnishing

For a flavor plus and professional finish, cover your ham choice with a glaze for the last 30 to 50 minutes of baking. One of our favorites is a mixture of 1 can (6 ounces) thawed frozen concentrated orange juice, 1 cup honey and 1 teaspoon Worcestershire sauce. This amount makes enough for a 10- to 14-pound ham. (Halve all ingredients for a smaller size.) To keep any of these trims fresh-looking, add them after the meat comes from the oven; glaze will be sticky enough to hold them in place.

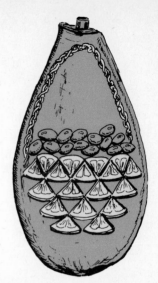

Have trouble making even cuts when scoring a ham? Use this simple string-and-wooden-pick guide. Place it diagonally across meat for diamonds or straight for squares, then stud each with a whole clove, if you wish.

A colorful Easter basket arranged on a whole ham catches the spirit of the day and is easy to put together. All you need are wedges of orange slices, candy-coated almonds or jelly beans and slender strips of orange peel to braid for the basket handle.

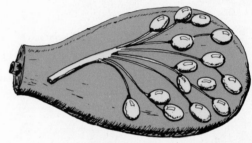

Spray of halved grapes and green-onion tops turns a big ham into a blossoming beauty. A few other choices for the petals; Halved preserved kumquats, thin radish rounds or maraschino-cherry halves.

Peach sunburst glitters invitingly atop a half ham. Place slices, overlapping, in a ring and center with a ruffle of almonds, pointed ends down, and a maraschino cherry.

Orange slices, flat and twisted, make an eye-catching garnish for ham steak. Group three slices for base; top each with another slice that has been slit just to center and overlapped. Hold in place with short wooden picks finished off with a perky cherry.

Carrot daisies look so springlike growing around a rolled boneless ham. To fix them, cut thin slices of raw carrot for petals and green pepper for leaves and stems.

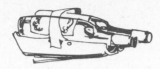

Madeira-Glazed Ham

Half ham, sensible choice for a small family, looks luxurious in its coat of brown sugar, mustard and wine.

Bake at 325° for 2 hours. Makes 8 servings plus enough for one bonus meal

1 fully cooked butt half ham, weighing about 7 pounds
½ cup firmly packed brown sugar
1 tablespoon dry mustard
¼ cup Madeira wine
¼ cup light corn syrup

1 Place ham on a rack in a large shallow baking pan. (Do not add water or cover pan.)
2 Bake in slow oven (325°) 1 hour; remove from oven. Trim off skin, if any; score fat into diamonds or squares with a sharp knife.
3 Mix brown sugar, mustard, wine and corn syrup in a small saucepan. Heat slowly, stirring constantly, until sugar dissolves; brush part over ham.
4 Continue baking, brushing several times with remaining sugar mixture, 1 hour, or until richly glazed. Remove to a heated large serving platter; garnish platter with canned minted pineapple cubes, if you wish. Carve ham into ¼-inch-thick slices.

Glazed Ham Seville

Bake at 325° for 2 hours. Makes 8 generous servings, plus enough for at least one bonus meal

1 fully cooked ham, weighing about 10 pounds
1 can (6 ounces) frozen concentrate for orange juice, thawed
¾ cup orange marmalade
2 whole pimientos
Green-onion tops
Watercress
SWEET-POTATO ACCORDIONS (recipe follows)

1 Place ham, fat side up, on a rack in a large shallow baking pan. (Do not add water or cover pan.)
2 Bake in slow oven (325°) 1½ hours; remove from oven. Trim off skin, if any.
3 Mix orange-juice concentrate and marmalade in a small bowl; brush part over ham.
4 Continue baking, brushing several times with remaining marmalade mixture, 30 minutes, or

1612

until richly glazed. Place ham on a heated large serving platter.
5 Place pimientos flat on a cutting board; carefully make sawtooth cuts in tops to resemble tulips. Cut green-onion tops into varying lengths for flower stems. Press pimientos and onion tops into glaze on ham to form a spray of flowers. If needed, hold pimientos in place with short pieces of wooden picks. Garnish platter with bouquets of watercress. Carve ham; serve with SWEET-POTATO ACCORDIONS.

SWEET-POTATO ACCORDIONS—Pare 8 medium size sweet potatoes; cut each potato crosswise into ¼-inch-thick slices almost to bottom. Grease a large baking dish. Arrange potatoes in a single layer in bottom of dish. Drizzle with ¼ cup water; dot with 4 tablespoons (½ stick) butter or margarine. Sprinkle with salt and pepper; cover. Bake in slow oven (325°) 1 hour and 30 minutes, or until tender. Makes 8 servings.

KNOW THE ART OF CARVING BAKED HAM

If you know where the bones are, it's easy to carve this handsome roast into big neat slices. Pictured steps show you how.

1 Place shank of ham to carver's right. If a left ham (above), cut a few slices from near side; for right, from far side.

2 Turn ham to rest on cut surface with rounded meaty part up, then cut a wedge-shape piece from shank end and lift out.

3 Start at wedge cut and slice meat—about ¼ inch thick—cutting down each time until knife touches the leg bone.

4 Cut slices from leg bone; lift onto platter. For seconds, turn ham back on side *(step one);* slice from other end.

Crumb-Topped Smithfield Ham

In Smithfield County in Virginia, the hams have been cured in a special way to give them a flavor all their own. This is a ham to be enjoyed in thin, thin slivers with buttered hot biscuits or corn bread. Wonderful for a buffet party.
Bake at 350° for 1 hour. Makes 16 servings, plus leftovers.

1 whole Smithfield ham, weighing about 14 pounds
  OR: 1 whole country-cured ham
½ cup light molasses
2 cups soft white bread crumbs (4 slices)

1 Soak ham overnight, or even 24 hours, in a large quanity of water. (If you have a free sink, that is the perfect place to soak the ham. This helps to remove some of the curing salt from the ham.)
2 Scrub the ham with a brush and rinse well to remove the pepper coating.
3 Place ham in a pan large enough to hold it and cover with cold water. (If this is impossible, fit ham, shank end up, in the largest roaster or kettle that you have and fill container with cold water. Wrap heavy duty foil around shank and up over kettle or roaster to cover.) Heat water to simmering, but do not boil. (South-

erners say that boiling water drives the salt into the ham.)
4 Simmer ham, turning every 2 hours, 6 hours, or until a meat thermometer inserted into the thickest part of the ham reaches 160°.
5 Remove ham from water; cool. Refrigerate until ready to prepare.
6 Place ham in a shallow roasting pan; remove rind; trim fat; score remaining fat. Brush with part of the molasses.
7 Bake in moderate oven (350°) 30 minutes. Brush ham with remaining molasses and pat bread crumbs onto ham. Bake 30 minutes longer, or until crumbs are golden.
8 Cut ham into very thin slices, holding the carving knife almost parallel to the bone, starting at the shank end.

Ham en Croûte with Jubilee Sauce

Spicy wine marinade, pastry crust and sauce of dark cherries make much of canned ham.
Bake at 400° for 1 hour. Makes 12 to 16 servings

1 five-pound canned ham
1 cup port wine
1 teaspoon pumpkin-pie spice
1 package piecrust mix
1 egg
1 tablespoon water
½ cup sugar
3 tablespoons cornstarch
1 can (1 pound) pitted dark sweet cherries

1 Scrape gelatin coating from ham into a small saucepan and set aside for next step. Pierce ham all over with a long metal skewer; place in a deep bowl just large enough to hold ham.
2 Add wine and pumpkin-pie spice to gelatin; heat just to boiling. Pour over ham; cover. Chill overnight.
3 Remove ham from marinade; pat dry with paper toweling. Set marinade aside for Step 8. (If marinade has set, place bowl in a pan of hot water until gelatin melts.)
4 Prepare piecrust mix, following label directions. Roll out to a rectangle, 16x12, on a lightly floured pastry cloth or board. Place ham in center of pastry; wrap pastry around ham, trimming off any excess; set trims aside for Step 6.
5 Beat egg slightly with water in a cup; brush part over edges of pastry; pinch edges to seal.
6 Place ham, seam-side down, on a large cookie sheet; brush all over with egg mixture. Cut pastry trims into flower shapes with a truffle cutter; arrange on top of ham; brush cutouts with egg mixture.
7 Bake in hot oven (400°) 1 hour, or until pastry

1613

is golden. Remove with pancake turners to a heated large serving platter.

8 While ham bakes, mix sugar and cornstarch in a medium-size saucepan; stir in saved marinade and syrup from cherries. Cook, stirring constantly, until sauce thickens and boils 3 minutes; stir in cherries. Carve ham into ¼-inch-thick slices; spoon cherry sauce over each.

Baked Ham in Cheese Crust
Bake at 325° for 2 hours and 30 minutes. Makes 12 servings

- 1 fully cooked boneless ham, weighing about 8 pounds
- 1 cup fine dry bread crumbs
- 1 cup shredded Swiss cheese (4 ounces)
- 2 tablespoons dry mustard
- 6 tablespoons (¾ stick), butter or margarine, melted
- ½ cup drained crushed pineapple (from an about-8-ounce can)

1 Place ham, fat side up, on a rack in a large shallow roasting pan (do not add water or cover pan).

2 Bake in slow oven (325°) for 2 hours; remove from oven; cool slightly.

3 Combine crumbs, cheese, mustard, melted butter or margarine and pineapple in a small bowl. Pat mixture firmly over top of ham. Return to oven.

4 Bake 30 minutes longer, or until cheese mixture is toasty brown.

5 Garnish ham with pimiento and watercress, if you wish.

Parisian Pork
Budget-wise picnic shoulder braises tasty and tender in vegetable-seasoned broth.
Makes 6 servings

- 1 smoked picnic shoulder, weighing about 5 pounds
- 2 large onions, chopped (2 cups)
- 2 cups chopped celery

Want an unusual way to dress up a boneless ham? Try Baked Ham in Cheese Crust. It's impressive but easy.

1 cup chopped pared carrot
2 cloves of garlic, minced
¼ cup chopped parsley
1 teaspoon leaf thyme, crumbled
¼ teaspoon seasoned pepper
1 cup water

1 Peel wrapping from pork; trim off skin and excess fat. Brown pork slowly in a Dutch oven or electric skillet; remove and set aside.
2 Stir onions, celery, carrot and garlic into drippings in pan; sauté until soft. Stir in parsley, thyme, seasoned pepper and water; return meat to Dutch oven; cover.
3 Simmer, turning meat once or twice, 2½ hours, or until tender. Remove to a heated large serving platter; keep warm while making gravy.
4 Let liquid in Dutch oven stand several minutes until fat rises to top, then skim off. Pour liquid into an electric-blender container; cover; beat until smooth. (Or strain liquid into a bowl, pressing vegetables through sieve.) Return to Dutch oven; heat just to boiling.
5 Carve pork into ¼-inch-thick slices; serve gravy separately to spoon over meat.

Ham Caribbean

Bake at 325° for 2 hours. Makes 8 servings, plus enough for two bonus meals

1 fully cooked boneless ham, weighing about 8 pounds
¼ cup port wine
¼ cup lime juice
¼ cup honey
2 tablespoons vegetable oil

1 Peel covering from ham; place ham on a rack in a shallow baking pan. Do not add water or cover.
2 Bake in slow oven (325°) 1½ hours; remove from oven. Score top.
3 Mix wine, lime juice, honey and vegetable oil in a small bowl; brush part over ham.
4 Continue baking, brushing several times with remaining wine mixture, 30 minutes, or until richly glazed. Place on a heated serving platter; frame with sprigs of parsley and thin lime slices, if you wish. Let stand 20 minutes.

Bavarian Baked Ham

Bake at 350° for 1 hour and 15 minutes. Makes 12 servings

1 five-pound canned ham
  Whole cloves
1 cup golden raisins
1 can (12 ounces) beer

¼ cup molasses
3 tablespoons brown sugar
2 tablespoons cornstarch
¼ cup water

1 Place ham in a shallow roasting pan. Score ham and stud with whole cloves. Place raisins in pan; pour beer over ham and raisins.
2 Bake in moderate oven (350°) 1 hour. Brush molasses over ham. Bake 15 minutes longer, or until ham is golden. Place ham on heated platter; keep warm.
3 Heat pan drippings and raisins to boiling. Combine brown sugar, cornstarch and water in a cup. Stir into drippings. Cook, stirring constantly, until mixture thickens and bubbles 1 minute. Serve with ham.

Budget Boiled Dinner

Sweet smoky pork plus four vegetables make this meal on a platter.
Makes 6 servings

1 smoked boneless cottage roll or butt (about 3 pounds)
2 tablespoons brown sugar
1 tablespoon mixed pickling spices
6 medium-size fresh beets
6 medium-size potatoes, pared
12 small carrots, scraped
1 small cabbage, cut into 6 wedges (about 1 pound)
  HORSERADISH-MUSTARD SAUCE (recipe follows)

1 Place cottage roll, brown sugar and pickling spices in a kettle; add water to cover; cover. Simmer 1¼ hours, or just until meat is tender.
2 Cut leafy tops about 1 inch from beets. (This helps beets keep their deep rich color.) Cook beets in boiling salted water in a medium-size saucepan 45 minutes, or until tender; drain. Run under cold water; slip off skins. Cut beets in quarters; return to saucepan; keep hot.
3 While beets cook, lay potatoes and carrots around mat in kettle; cover; cook 30 minutes. Place cabbage wedges on top; cook 15 minutes longer, or until all vegetables are tender.
4 Lift out vegetables with a slotted spoon; place in separate mounds around edge of a heated large serving platter. (Slice carrots, if you wish.)
5 Slice part of cottage roll; place all in middle of platter. Serve with HORSERADISH-MUSTARD SAUCE.
  HORSERADISH-MUSTARD SAUCE—Blend 1 cup dairy sour cream, 2 tablespoons prepared horseradish, 2 teaspoons dry mustard and 1 teaspoon salt in a small bowl; cover. Chill. Makes about 1 cup.

1615

ROASTS: THE COMEBACK TRAIL

ROASTS ON THE COMEBACK TRAIL: WHAT TO DO WITH LEFTOVER ROAST BEEF, VEAL, LAMB, PORK AND HAM

It isn't difficult for yesterday's roast (or last week's) to stage a beautiful comeback. Every roast can and *should*—it's far too luxurious a cut to be sliced and slipped cold into uninspired sandwiches.

Instead, try turning the rest of the roast into an exciting main dish or an imaginative salad so that the family actually looks forward to the leftovers. Or, better still, doesn't *recognize* them.

Roasts can be every bit as good the second or third time around as they were the first. Magic? Not really. It's more a matter of good management. Of planning ahead. To prove the point, herewith, a portfolio of recipes *planned* specifically for leftover roasts. *Planned-overs,* we call them, not leftovers. There are recipes showing how to use neat slices of cold roast to best advantage, how to make the most of chunks and slivers, even how to put the bones to good use.

Utilizing every scrap of roast makes *sense.* Better spell that *cents,* because a clever use of leftovers adds up to many main dishes from one big roast.

All roasts revisited (leftovers, that is). Left to right: Boeuf à la Mode en Gelée, Sweet and Pungent Pork and Savory Stuffed Cabbage filled with lamb.

WHAT TO DO WITH LEFTOVER ROAST BEEF

Boeuf à la Mode en Gelée
Makes 6 servings

- 3 medium carrots, pared and cut in ½-inch slices
- 1 pint Brussels sprouts, washed and trimmed
- 2 cans (10½ ounces each) condensed beef broth
- 1⅓ cups water
- 2 envelopes unflavored gelatin
- 3 tablespoons Madeira or dry sherry
- 6 drops liquid red pepper seasoning
- 1 pound cooked roast beef or steak, sliced thin
  Watercress
  HORSERADISH DRESSING (recipe follows)

1617

1 Cook carrots and Brussels sprouts separately in boiling salted water 15 minutes or until tender. Drain; chill.
2 Combine beef broth and water in medium-size bowl. Soften gelatin in 1 cup of broth, about 5 minutes, in a small saucepan. Heat, stirring constantly, until gelatin dissolves; stir into remaining broth in bowl. Add Madeira and red pepper seasoning. Cut Brussels sprouts in half lengthwise.

3 Pour ¾ cup of the gelatin mixture into an 11x7x1½-inch pan or an 8-cup shallow mold; place in a larger pan of ice and water until gelatin is sticky-firm. Arrange part of the Brussels sprouts and carrots in decorative pattern along sides of pan. Make 12 rolls or bundles of meat slices; place 6 down center of pan, spacing evenly; spoon several tablespoons of remaining gelatin mixture over vegetables and meat. Arrange some of remaining Brussels sprouts against sides of pan. Add enough gelatin mixture to almost cover meat. Chill until sticky-firm.
4 Arrange remaining meat and vegetables on top of first layer in pan; set pan on shelf in refrigerator; carefully spoon remaining gelatin over to cover meat and vegetables completely. Chill until firm, several hours or overnight.
5 Just before serving, loosen gelatin around edges with a knife; dip pan quickly in and out of hot water; wipe off water. Cover pan with serving plate; turn upside down; shake gently; lift off mold. Border with watercress, if you wish. Serve with HORSERADISH DRESSING.

HORSERADISH DRESSING—Combine ¾ cup mayonnaise or salad dressing; 1 hard-cooked egg, sieved; 1 tablespoon tarragon vinegar; and 1 teaspoon prepared horseradish in a small bowl; stir to blend well. Cover; refrigerate to blend flavors. Makes 1 cup.

●

Deviled Beef Slices
Everyone will love second-day beef when it's served this way.
Makes 4 servings

8 slices cooked beef (¼-inch thick)
2 tablespoons prepared mustard
1 egg

1618

Cool summer leftover: Medallion of Beef Platter.

½ teaspoon salt
Few drops red pepper seasoning
2 tablespoons water
1 cup seasoned fine dry bread crumbs
4 tablespoons vegetable oil

1 Spread beef slices with prepared mustard.
2 Beat egg in a pie plate. Stir in salt, red pepper seasoning and water. Sprinkle bread crumbs on wax paper.
3 Dip beef slices first into seasoned egg and then into bread crumbs.
4 Heat oil in a large skillet. Brown beef slices on one side; turn and brown on second side. Serve on a heated platter.

Beef in Horseradish Sauce
Makes 6 servings

1 cup chopped celery
1 medium-size onion, chopped (½ cup)
2 tablespoons butter or margarine
1 teaspoon curry powder
½ teaspoon ground ginger
½ teaspoon pepper
1 can (about 11 ounces) beef gravy
¼ cup dry red wine
1 tablespoon Worcestershire sauce
1 teaspoon prepared horseradish
3 cups diced roast beef
1 cup (8-ounce carton) dairy sour cream
1 tablespoon chopped parsley
Mashed potatoes

1 Sauté celery and onion in butter or margarine until soft in a large frying pan.
2 Stir in curry powder, ginger and pepper; cook 1 to 2 minutes. Stir in gravy, wine, Worcestershire sauce, horseradish, and beef; heat to boiling; cover. Simmer 10 minutes to blend flavors.
3 Stir about 1 cupful of the hot sauce into sour cream in a small bowl, then stir back into meat mixture in pan. Heat slowly until hot; stir in parsley. Serve over mashed potatoes.

●

Medallion of Beef Platter
Makes 6 servings

2 packages (10 ounces each) frozen succotash
½ cup thinly sliced celery
3 green onions, trimmed and sliced (about ½ cup)

¼ cup chopped pimientos
½ cup bottled oil-and-vinegar salad dressing
½ teaspoon salt
¼ teaspoon leaf marjoram, crumbled
1 large firm ripe tomato
½ cup mayonnaise or salad dressing
2 tablespoons prepared horseradish-mustard
1 teaspoon lemon juice
  Paprika
  Boston lettuce
12 thin slices roast beef, rolled up

1 Cook succotash, following label directions; drain. Combine with celery, green onions and pimientos in a shallow dish. Drizzle salad dressing over vegetables, then sprinkle salt and marjoram over top; toss lightly to mix. Chill at least an hour to season.
2 Cut a thick slice from stem end of tomato; scoop out inside; cut a sawtooth edge around top, if you wish. Turn tomato upside down on paper toweling to drain.
3 Blend mayonnaise or salad dressing, horseradish-mustard and lemon juice in a small bowl; spoon into tomato; sprinkle with paprika.
4 When ready to serve, line a large round platter with lettuce; spoon vegetable mixture in a layer over lettuce. Arrange beef rolls, pinwheel fashion, on top; place tomato in center.

Cornish Beef Hash and Egg Pie
An old favorite all dressed up in a flaky pastry crust, topped with eggs that cook right inside the pie.
Bake at 450° for 10 minutes, then at 400° for 20 minutes. Makes 6 servings

  3 medium-size onions, chopped (1½ cups)
  2 tablespoons butter or margarine
2½ cups chopped cooked corned beef (¾ pound)
  3 cups chopped boiled potatoes
  1 teaspoon Worcestershire sauce
  ½ teaspoon salt
  ¼ teaspoon pepper
  1 package piecrust mix
  ¼ cup milk
  6 eggs

1 Sauté onion in butter or margarine until soft in medium-size skillet, about 5 minutes.
2 Combine corned beef, potatoes, onions, Worcestershire sauce, salt and pepper in a large bowl, toss to mix well with a fork.
3 Prepare piecrust mix, following label directions or make pastry from your favorite two-crust recipe. Roll out ½ of pastry to a 12-inch round on a lightly floured board; fit into a 9-inch, deep pie plate. Trim overhang to ½ inch.
4 Spoon hash mixture into prepared pastry shell; mounding center higher than sides Scoop a hollow about 1½ inches wide, 1 inch in from edge all around. Drizzle milk over hash. Break eggs into hollow, spacing evenly.
5 Roll out remaining pastry to an 11-inch round; cut several slits near center to let steam escape; cover pie. Trim overhang to ½ inch; turn edge under, flush with rim; flute edge. Roll out trimmings to make fancy cutouts for top, if you wish. Brush top and cutouts with milk.
6 Bake in very hot oven (450°) for 10 minutes, reduce heat to 400° and bake 15 minutes longer, or until pastry is golden. Cut into wedges and serve hot.

Beefeater Sandwiches
Build these knife-and-fork whoppers with beef slices, gravy, asparagus and onion rings atop toasty English muffins.
Makes 6 servings

  1 package (10 ounces) frozen asparagus spears
12 thin slices cooked roast beef
  1 can (about 11 ounces) beef gravy blended with ½ cup water
  4 tablespoons (½ stick) butter or margarine
  2 tablespoons prepared horseradish
  6 English muffins, split
  1 can (about 3 ounces) French fried onion rings

1 Cook asparagus, following label directions; drain; keep hot.
2 Trim all fat from beef slices; place in large frying pan; pour gravy over. Cover; heat slowly just until gravy bubbles and meat is piping-hot.
3 Blend butter or margarine with horseradish in a cup; set aside for Step 5.
4 Place muffin halves on broiler rack; toast on both sides; turn off heat. Spread onion rings in shallow baking pan; slide into oven to crisp. (Oven will be hot enough after broiler is turned off.)
5 Spread toasted muffin halves with horseradish butter; place 2 on each serving plate. Top with sliced beef and asparagus, dividing evenly. Spoon gravy over; sprinkle generously with onion rings.

SOME WAYS TO USE LEFTOVER ROAST VEAL

A most palatable palette: Mediterranean Veal Salad.

Mediterranean Veal Salad
Makes 6 servings

3 cups thin strips roast veal
½ cup bottled herb-and-garlic French dressing
6 medium-size potatoes, pared and sliced
1 cup finely chopped celery
2 tablespoons minced onion
½ cup mayonnaise or salad dressing
   Romaine
¼ cup diced pimientos
¼ cup quartered pitted ripe olives
1 small onion, peeled, sliced and separated into rings
   Chopped parsley

1 Combine veal and ¼ cup of the French dressing in a medium-size bowl; chill 2 to 3 hours to season.
2 Cook potatoes, covered, in boiling salted water in a large saucepan 15 minutes, or until tender; drain. Combine with celery and minced onion in a medium-size bowl; drizzle with remaining ¼ cup French dressing; toss lightly to mix. Fold in mayonnaise or salad dressing; spoon into a 6-cup bowl, pressing mixture down lightly with back of spoon. Chill at least an hour.
3 When ready to serve, line a large platter with romaine; unmold potato salad into center. Arrange veal in sections around potato salad; place pimientos, olives and onion rings in between. Sprinkle chopped parsley in a ribbon over potato salad, if you wish.

French Veal Puff
Whisk it right from oven to table so everyone can see its golden crown.
Bake at 350° for 45 minutes. Makes 6 servings

3 slices bacon, cut in 1-inch pieces
2 tablespoons all-purpose flour
1 teaspoon salt
½ teaspoon leaf basil, crumbled
¼ teaspoon pepper
¼ teaspoon leaf thyme, crumbled
2 cups milk
½ cup soft bread crumbs (1 slice)
2 cups ground roast veal
2 tablespoons finely chopped shallots or onion
4 eggs, separated
   PIQUANT CREAM SAUCE (recipe follows)

1 Prepare a 4-cup straight-side baking dish this way: Fold a piece of foil, long enough to go around dish and overlap slightly, in half lengthwise. Butter strip; dust evenly with flour; wrap around dish, butter side in, to make a 3-inch stand-up collar; hold in place with paper clip and string.
2 Sauté bacon just until crisp in large saucepan; remove and drain on paper toweling for Step 4.
3 Pour off all drippings into a cup; return 2 tablespoonfuls to saucepan. Blend in flour, salt, basil, pepper and thyme; cook, stirring all the time, just until mixture bubbles.
4 Stir in milk slowly; continue cooking and stirring until sauce thickens and boils 1 minute. Beat in bread crumbs until mixture is well blended; remove from heat. Stir in veal, shallots or onion and bacon.
5 Beat egg whites until they form soft peaks in large bowl.
6 Beat egg yolks slightly in small bowl; blend in a few spoonfuls hot meat mixture, then quickly stir back into mixture in saucepan; cool to lukewarm.
7 Fold gently into beaten egg whites until no streaks of white remain. Pour into prepared dish.
8 Set baking dish in pan; place on oven shelf; pour boiling water into pan to depth of 1 inch.
9 Bake in moderate oven (350°) 45 minutes, or until puffy-light and firm in center. Serve at once with PIQUANT CREAM SAUCE.
   PIQUANT CREAM SAUCE—Blend 1 can (about 11 ounces) chicken gravy, ⅓ cup milk and 1 tablespoon lemon juice in small saucepan; heat slowly just until bubbly. Makes about 1½ cups.

Dividend Blanquette of Veal
Makes 6 servings

12 small onions, peeled
3 large carrots, pared and sliced
1 bay leaf
   Few sprigs parsley

1620

1 cup dry white wine
2 cans (about 14 ounces each) chicken broth
4 green onions, trimmed and chopped
1 clove of garlic, minced
2 stalks celery, sliced
12 medium-size fresh mushrooms, trimmed and sliced
6 tablespoons (¾ stick) butter or margarine
½ cup sifted all-purpose flour
¼ teaspoon leaf thyme, crumbled
2 tablespoons lemon juice
3 cups diced roast veal
2 egg yolks
1 cup cream

1 Combine small onions, carrots, bay leaf, parsley, white wine and chicken broth in a large saucepan; heat to boiling. Simmer 20 minutes; remove from heat. Pour off liquid into a medium-size bowl.
2 Sauté green onions, garlic, celery and mushrooms in butter or margarine until soft in a kettle. Sprinkle flour and thyme over top, then stir in with liquid from vegetables and lemon juice. Cook slowly, stirring constantly, 10 minutes.
3 Discard bay leaf and parsley from vegetables. Stir vegetables and veal into sauce; heat to boiling; simmer 5 minutes. (Do not boil.)
4 Beat egg yolks with cream in a small bowl; stir in about 1 cupful of the hot sauce, then stir back into mixture in kettle. Heat slowly, stirring constantly, until hot. Season with salt and pepper, and serve over rice, if you wish.

SOME LUSCIOUS LAMB LEFTOVERS

South Seas Lamb Supper
Makes 6 servings

¾ cup uncooked regular rice
2 tablespoons chopped parsley
¼ cup bottled oil-and-vinegar salad dressing
3 cups diced roast lamb
1 cup thinly sliced celery
¾ cup mayonnaise or salad dressing
2 tablespoons chopped chutney
1 tablespoon minced onion
2 teaspoons curry powder
   Lemon juice
1 red apple

1 Cook rice, following label directions; place in a large bowl. Sprinkle parsley and oil-and-vinegar dressing over top; toss lightly to mix. Chill.
2 Combine lamb and celery in a large bowl. Blend mayonnaise or salad dressing, chutney, onion, curry powder and ½ teaspoon lemon juice in a cup; spoon over lamb mixture; toss to mix.
3 When ready to serve, quarter apple, core and slice thin crosswise. Dip slices in lemon juice to prevent darkening.
4 Spoon rice mixture in a ring on a large serving platter; spoon lamb mixture in center. Overlap apple slices around edge. Garnish with several slices of hard-cooked egg and parsley.

●

Savory Stuffed Cabbage
Bake at 350° for 1 hour and 30 minutes. Makes 6 servings

1 pound roast lamb, ground
2 cups cooked rice
1 egg
1 clove garlic, crushed
1 teaspoon salt
¼ teaspoon leaf thyme, crumbled
¼ teaspoon leaf rosemary, crumbled
⅛ teaspoon pepper
1 can (15 ounces) tomato sauce
1 head of cabbage (about 3½ pounds)
2 tablespoons butter or margarine
1 large onion, chopped (1 cup)
2 teaspoons sugar
½ teaspoon salt
½ cup water

1 Combine lamb, rice, egg, garlic, salt, thyme, rosemary, pepper and ⅔ cup of the tomato sauce in large bowl; mix well with fork.

South Seas Lamb Supper.

1621

2 Trim outside leaves from cabbage. Cut a small slice about 3 inches in diameter from top end; set aside. With a sharp-tip knife and hands, hollow out cabbage leaving a shell about ½ inch thick. (Chop cut-out pieces coarsely and cook separately to serve along with stuffed cabbage or save to cook as a vegetable for another day.)
3 Spoon lamb mixture into shell, pressing it down firmly, fit top back into place; tie with a string.
4 Sauté onion in hot butter or margarine in medium-size frying pan until soft, about 5 minutes; add remaining tomato sauce, sugar, salt, and water. Bring to boiling, stirring constantly. Remove from heat.
5 Place cabbage, core end down, in a deep flameproof casserole or Dutch oven; pour sauce over; cover. (If cabbage is too high, use an inverted bowl or foil to cover.)
6 Bake in moderate oven (350°), basting 2 or 3 times with sauce, for 1 hour and 30 minutes.
7 Place stuffed cabbage on a heated serving platter; remove string. Spoon some of sauce over cabbage; pass remaining sauce in a separate bowl. Cut cabbage into wedges for serving. Garnish with parsley, if you wish.
Serving Idea—Save several of the pretty large outer cabbage leaves. Blanch them in boiling salted water, just before cabbage is served, then wrap leaves around cabbage before serving.

Oven-Baked Lamb Curry
Bake at 350° for 1½ hours. Makes 6 servings

    2 tablespoons butter or margarine
    1 tablespoon curry powder
 1½ pounds cubed lamb shoulder
    1 large onion, chopped (1 cup)
    1 cup chopped celery
    1 green pepper, halved, seeded and chopped
    1 envelope instant chicken broth
      OR: 1 teaspoon granulated chicken bouillon
   ¼ cup water
    1 cup plain yogurt
    1 teaspoon salt
      Hot cooked rice

1622

1 Melt butter or margarine in a large heavy skillet. Stir in curry powder and cook 1 minute. Add lamb and brown well. Remove with a slotted spoon to an 8-cup baking dish.
2 Sauté onion, celery and green pepper until soft in pan drippings. Add instant chicken broth and water. Cover skillet. Simmer 5 minutes.
3 Cool mixture slightly and place in electric-blender container. Whirl until smooth. (Or purée through a food mill.)

4 Combine vegetable mixture, yogurt and salt in a medium-size bowl. Pour over lamb in baking dish and cover.
5 Bake in moderate oven (350°) 1½ hours, or until lamb is tender when pierced with fork. Serve with rice.

Lamb Indonesia
Thin slices of cooked lamb, brushed with a soy-garlic sauce, broil crispy brown.
Makes 4 servings

    1 cup water
   ½ cup soy sauce
   ¼ cup sugar
    1 chicken-bouillon cube
    1 clove of garlic
   12 thin slices cold roast lamb

1 Combine all ingredients, except lamb, in small saucepan; cover. Heat to boiling; simmer 15 minutes to blend flavors.
2 Arrange lamb slices in single layer on broiler rack. Brush generously with soy mixture.
3 Broil about 4 inches from heat, brushing often with more sauce, 5 minutes on each side, or until very brown and crisp. Serve with buttered hot noodles, if you wish.

Easter Monday Lamb Platter
Slices of meat are breaded and browned, then served with warm horseradish sauce.
Makes 4 servings

    1 egg
    1 teaspoon salt
   ½ teaspoon basil leaves, crumbled
      Water
   ¾ cup fine dry bread crumbs
    8 thin slices roast lamb
    3 tablespoons butter or margarine
    1 tablespoon all-purpose flour
   ½ cup dairy sour cream
    1 tablespoon prepared horseradish
    1 package (10 ounces) frozen lima beans, cooked and drained

1 Beat egg with ½ teaspoon of the salt, basil and 2 tablespoons water in a pie plate; place bread crumbs in a second pie plate.
2 Dip lamb slices into egg mixture, then into bread crumbs to coat well. Brown, a few at a time, in butter or margarine in a large frying pan; remove all and keep warm while making sauce.

3 Stir flour and remaining ½ teaspoon salt into drippings in frying pan; cook, stirring constantly, just until bubbly. Stir in ¾ cup water; continue cooking and stirring until sauce thickens and boils 1 minute. Stir into sour cream in a small bowl; return to frying pan.
4 Stir in horseradish. Heat slowly just until hot, but do not let sauce boil.
5 Spoon lima beans onto a heated serving platter; overlap lamb slices in a row on top. Drizzle with several spoonfuls of the sauce; garnish with a sprinkle of paprika, if you wish. Serve the remaining sauce separately.

Sweet-Sour Lamb
Use any bits and pieces of meat to fix this saucy Chinese-style dish.
Makes 4 servings

    1 can (1 pound) tomatoes
    ⅓ cup firmly packed brown sugar
    2 tablespoons cider vinegar
    1 teaspoon soy sauce
    2 tablespoons cornstarch
    ¼ cup water
    ½ cup diced sweet mixed pickles
    1 large green pepper, halved, seeded and cut
      in ¼-inch-wide strips
    2 cups bite-size pieces roast lamb
      Chinese noodles

1 Combine tomatoes, brown sugar, vinegar and soy sauce in a large saucepan.
2 Mix cornstarch and water until smooth in a cup; stir into tomato mixture. Cook, stirring constantly, until sauce thickens and boils 3 minutes.
3 Stir in pickles, green-pepper strips and lamb; heat, stirring constantly, to boiling. Serve over crisp Chinese noodles.

Tureen Supper
Simmer the bone from your roast for savory broth, then add a few hearty extras.
Makes 6 to 8 servings

    1 package (1 pound) dried split green peas
    6 cups boiling water
    2 tablespoons butter or margarine
    4 cups shredded cabbage (about 1 pound)
    1 large onion, chopped (1 cup)
    1 cup chopped celery
    1 clove garlic, minced

    1 lamb bone (from roast lamb)
    1 package (12 ounces) smoked sausage
      links, sliced thin
    2½ teaspoons salt
    ¾ teaspoon pepper
    ½ teaspoon Italian seasoning

1 Combine peas and boiling water in a large bowl; cover. Let stand 1 hour.
2 Melt butter or margarine in a kettle or Dutch oven; stir in cabbage, onion, celery and garlic. Sauté slowly, stirring often, 20 minutes.
3 Pour peas and liquid into kettle; add lamb bone, sausage, seasonings and another 6 cups water. Heat to boiling; cover. Simmer 1½ hours.
4 Remove lamb bone from kettle; let cool until easy to handle, then strip off any bits of meat and return to kettle; cover again.
5 Simmer 45 minutes longer, or until peas are tender. Ladle into heated soup bowls or plates.

Lamb-Eggplant Puffs
Soufflélike lamb filling, lightly seasoned with curry, bakes beautifully in scooped-out eggplants.
Bake at 350° for 1 hour. Makes 6 servings

    2 medium-size eggplants (about 1½ pounds
      each)
    1 package (6 ounces) sliced salami
    1 tablespoon butter or margarine
    2 tablespoons chopped onion
    ½ teaspoon curry powder
    1½ cups soft whole-wheat bread crumbs (3
      slices)
    1 teaspoon mixed salad herbs
    ½ cup light cream or table cream
    4 eggs
    2 cups finely diced roast lamb
    1 teaspoon salt
    ¼ cup minced pistachio or piñon nuts
      Parsley

1 Cut a 1-inch-thick slice lengthwise from each eggplant; pare slices and dice pulp. Cut pulp from eggplants in big chunks, leaving a ¼-inch-thick shell; dice pulp. (There should be about 8 cups.) Place shells in a greased shallow baking dish for Step 5.
2 Cook pulp in boiling salted water in a large saucepan, covered, 15 minutes, or until very soft; *drain well.* (Pulp will now measure about 1½ cups.) Set aside for Step 5.
3 Halve 3 slices of the salami; dice remaining.

Sauté slices lightly in butter or margarine in a medium-size frying pan; remove and set aside for garnish. Stir diced salami, onion and curry powder into drippings in pan. Sauté, stirring often, 3 minutes, or until onion is soft; remove from heat.

4 Stir in bread crumbs, salad herbs, and cream until well blended.

5 Separate eggs, placing yolks in a large bowl and whites in a medium-size bowl. Beat egg whites just until they form soft peaks. Beat egg yolks until creamy-thick; beat in crumb mixture; stir in cooked eggplant, lamb and salt; fold in beaten egg whites. Spoon into eggplant shells; sprinkle with nuts.

6 Bake in moderate oven (350°) 1 hour, or until puffy-firm and golden. Place on a heated serving platter.

7 Roll saved salami slices into cornucopia shapes; fasten with wooden picks; place a sprig of parsley in each. Tuck around eggplants on platter. To serve, spoon soufflé from eggplant shells, topping each serving with a salami cornucopia.

Romaine Roll-Ups

Each little bundle hides an herb-lamb filling. Topper is a mellow mushroom gravy.
Makes 4 to 6 servings

- 2 tablespoons butter or margarine
- 2 tablespoons all-purpose flour
- 1 teaspoon salt
- ¼ teaspoon pepper
- ¼ teaspoon leaf thyme, crumbled
- 1 envelope instant chicken broth
  OR: 1 chicken-bouillon cube
- 1 cup water
- 3 cups ground roast lamb
- 1 can (1 pound, 13 ounces) hominy, drained
- 16 large romaine leaves (from 1 or 2 heads)
- 1 can (about 11 ounces) mushroom gravy
- 1 can (8 ounces) tomato sauce

1624

1 Melt butter or margarine in a large saucepan; stir in flour, salt, pepper and thyme; cook, stirring constantly, until bubbly. Stir in chicken broth or bouillon cube and water; continue cooking, stirring constantly, until sauce is very thick and boils 1 minute; remove from heat. Stir in lamb and hominy; cool while preparing romaine.

2 Wash romaine leaves; trim off about an inch from bottom, then pare down ridge of each rib so leaf can be rolled easily. Dip leaves, 2 or 3 at a time, in boiling water for about 15 seconds to soften; lift out and spread flat on paper toweling to dry.

3 Spoon about ¼ cup of the meat filling onto

each leaf about an inch from bottom. Fold bottom up over filling, then fold both sides toward middle and roll up to cover filling completely; fasten with one or two wooden picks.

4 Place rolls in a single layer on a rack in a large pan. Pour in water almost to bottom of rack; cover tightly.

5 Steam 15 minutes, or until romaine is tender and filling is hot.

6 While rolls cook, combine mushroom gravy and tomato sauce in a small saucepan; heat, stirring often, to boiling.

7 Place rolls on a heated large serving platter; top with several spoonfuls of the sauce, then serve remaining separately.

Shepherd's Stew

So fresh-tasting! Leftover cubed meat, simmered in a rich sauce, is served in fluffy potato-carrot nests.
Makes 4 servings

- 2 cups cubed roast lamb
- 4 tablespoons all-purpose flour
- ½ teaspoon salt
  Dash of pepper
- 3 tablespoons vegetable oil
- 1 large onion, chopped (1 cup)
- 1 can (10½ ounces) condensed beef consommé
- ½ teaspoon rosemary leaves, crumbled
- 4 small potatoes, pared
- 4 large carrots, pared and cut in 1-inch-long pieces
- 1 package (9 ounces) frozen artichoke hearts

1 Shake lamb with flour, salt and pepper in a paper bag to coat evenly all over.

2 Brown in vegetable oil in a large frying pan; push to one side. Stir onion into drippings and sauté until soft.

3 Stir in consommé and rosemary; cover. Simmer 30 minutes.

4 While meat mixture simmers, cook potatoes and carrots in boiling salted water in a medium-size saucepan 20 minutes, or until tender; drain. Cook artichoke hearts, following label directions; drain. Stir into stew mixture.

5 Put potatoes and carrots through a ricer onto serving plates; hollow each mound with back

Veal is the Italian favorite, but lamb leftovers mix beautifully with eggplant in tomatoey Lamb Parmigiana.

of spoon to form a nest. Spoon stew mixture into hollows.

Lamb Parmigiana

Plan to have enough lamb left from a roast to make this bonus treat.

Bake at 350° for 1 hour. Makes 6 servings

4 tablespoons olive oil
1 large eggplant, pared and cut into ½-inch-thick slices
2 tablespoons water
1 large onion, chopped (1 cup)
1 clove garlic, minced
1 can (about 2 pounds) Italian tomatoes
1 tablespoon sugar
2 teaspoons salt
1 teaspoon mixed Italian herbs
¼ teaspoon pepper
4 tablespoons fine dry bread crumbs
3 cups cubed cooked lamb (about 1 pound)

1 package (8 ounces) sliced mozzarella or pizza cheese, cut into strips

1 Spoon 2 tablespoons olive oil into a large frying pan; arrange eggplant slices, slightly overlapping, in pan; drizzle remaining 2 tablespoons salad oil and water over. Cover; steam 15 minutes. Remove eggplant from pan and drain on paper toweling while making sauce.
2 Sauté onion and garlic until soft in same frying pan; stir in tomatoes, sugar, salt, Italian herbs and pepper, then simmer 5 minutes.
3 Arrange half of the eggplant slices in a 10-cup baking dish; sprinkle with 2 tablespoons bread crumbs. Top with half of the lamb and tomato sauce. Repeat with remaining eggplant, bread crumbs, meat and sauce.
4 Bake in moderate oven (350°) 45 minutes, or until mixture starts to bubble in center; crisscross cheese strips on top. Bake 15 minutes longer, or until cheese melts and is creamy-golden.

1625

HOW TO MAKE SOMETHING OF LEFTOVER ROAST PORK AND HAM

Molded Pork Loaf
Makes 6 generous servings

2 envelopes unflavored gelatin
1 tablespoon instant minced onion
1 bay leaf
2 cans (about 14 ounces each) chicken broth
¼ cup lemon juice
¼ teaspoon liquid red pepper seasoning
3 cups finely chopped roast pork
1 can (1 pound) sliced carrots, drained
1 can (1 pound) whole green beans, drained
1 can or jar (7 ounces) pimientos, drained and diced
1 large green pepper, halved, seeded and diced
Chicory or curly endive

1 Combine gelatin, onion, bay leaf and 1 can of the chicken broth in a small saucepan. Heat slowly, stirring constantly, until gelatin dissolves; strain into a medium-size bowl. Stir in remaining 1 can chicken broth, lemon juice and red pepper seasoning.
2 Measure out 1½ cups of the gelatin mixture and pour over pork in a small bowl; let stand until cool.
3 Place a loaf pan, 9x5x3, in a pan of ice and water to speed setting. Pour ½ cup of the plain gelatin mixture into loaf pan; chill just until as thick as unbeaten egg white.
4 Arrange about 12 carrot slices, 8 of the beans and a few pieces each pimiento and green pep-

1626

Cool Molded Pork Loaf is an appetizing work of art.

per in a pretty pattern in thickened gelatin; chill just until sticky-firm. Carefully spoon in about half of the gelatin-pork mixture. Chill again until sticky-firm.
5 Place remaining carrots and beans in a layer on top; spoon in enough more plain gelatin mixture to cover vegetables. Chill until sticky-firm, then add remaining pork mixture, pimientos, green pepper and plain gelatin mixture. Remove from ice and water. Chill in refrigerator several hours, or overnight, until firm.
6 When ready to serve, loosen loaf around edges with a knife; dip pan *very quickly* in and out of hot water. Cover with a serving platter; turn upside down; gently lift off pan. Garnish platter with chicory or curly endive. Cut loaf crosswise into slices.

●

Sweet and Pungent Pork
Makes 6 servings

3½ cups cooked pork (1¼ pounds), cut into ¾-inch cubes
1 tablespoon soy sauce
1 egg, slightly beaten
Oil for frying
½ cup cornstarch (for coating)
Sauce
1 large onion, chopped (1 cup)
1 large green pepper, halved, seeded and cut into strips
3 carrots, pared and sliced very thin (1 cup)
1 tablespoon vegetable oil
1 tablespoon cornstarch
1 cup water
5 tablespoons cider vinegar
¼ cup firmly packed light brown sugar
1 envelope or teaspoon instant chicken broth
1 can (about 13 ounces) pineapple tidbits

1 Combine pork with soy sauce in a medium-size bowl; toss to mix with fork; cover. Let stand at room temperature 30 minutes. Add egg, toss to coat meat well with egg.
2 Pour enough vegetable oil to make 1-inch depth in a medium-size skillet or saucepan; heat to 375° on deep-fat thermometer.
3 Place ½ cup cornstarch in a plastic bag; add pork cubes and shake bag until meat is well coated with cornstarch.
4 Sauté pork, about a third at a time, in the hot oil 3 minutes, or until golden brown and coating is crisp. Lift out with a slotted spoon; drain on paper toweling. Keep warm.
5 Sauté onion, green pepper and carrots in oil in large skillet 2 to 3 minutes, or until vegetables are crisply tender.
6 Mix 1 tablespoon cornstarch with 2 tablespoons water in cup. Add remaining water, vin-

egar, sugar and chicken broth to skillet; bring to boiling; cover; reduce heat; simmer 5 minutes. Stir in pineapple and cornstarch mixture; bring to boiling, stirring constantly; cover; cook just until thickened and bubbly, about 1 minute.
7 Just before serving, combine sauce with pork. Then serve with hot cooked rice and additional soy sauce, if you wish.

Skillet Pork-Rice
A quick and delicious way to use meat left from pork roast.
Makes 4 servings

- 2 cups finely diced lean roast pork (about 1 pound)
- 4 tablespoons vegetable oil
- 1 large onion, chopped (1 cup)
- 4 cups well-drained cold cooked rice (1 cup uncooked)
- 1 tablespoon soy sauce
- ¼ cup salted peanuts
- 2 eggs, slightly beaten
- 1 tablespoon chopped parsley

1 Brown pork lightly in 1 tablespoon of the vegetable oil in a large frying pan; remove with a slotted spoon to a small bowl. Stir in onion; sauté just until soft; add to pork in bowl. (Set aside for Step 3.)
2 Heat remaining 3 tablespoons vegetable oil in same frying pan; stir in rice. (Rice cooked the day before browns better than if freshly cooked.) Cook, stirring often, over medium heat 10 minutes, or just until grains separate and turn creamy-white.
3 Return pork and onion to pan; stir in soy sauce and peanuts. Drizzle beaten eggs over; fold over a few times until eggs are cooked.
4 Spoon into a heated serving bowl; sprinkle with parsley. Serve with additional soy sauce, if you wish.

Confetti Pork Bake
Layers of fluffy rice and lean pork bake in a creamy soup sauce.
Bake at 350° about 40 minutes. Makes 4 servings

- ¾ cup uncooked regular rice
- 1 package (10 ounces) frozen green peas
- ½ cup chopped celery
- 3 tablespoons butter or margarine
- 1 cup soft bread crumbs (2 slices)
- 1 medium-size onion, chopped (½ cup)

- 3 cups diced roast pork
- ½ teaspoon leaf marjoram, crumbled
- 1 can (10½ ounces) condensed cream of mushroom soup
- ¾ cup milk
- 1 pimiento, diced
- 1 tablespoon chopped parsley

1 Cook rice, following label directions, adding peas and celery during last 5 minutes' cooking.
2 Melt 1 tablespoon butter or margarine in medium-size frying pan; remove from heat; stir in bread crumbs; spoon into a cup and set aside for Step 5.
3 Sauté onion in remaining 2 tablespoons butter or margarine until softened in same frying pan; add pork and brown lightly. Stir in marjoram, mushroom soup and milk until well mixed.
4 Layer rice and meat mixtures into greased 8-cup casserole; top with saved buttered crumbs.
5 Bake in moderate oven (350°) 40 minutes, or until bubbly-hot. Sprinkle pimiento and parsley on top.

Island Pork Pie
Bake at 400° for 30 minutes. Makes 6 servings

- 1 medium-size onion, chopped (½ cup)
- ½ large green pepper, seeded and diced (½ cup)
- ½ cup thinly sliced celery
- 1 clove of garlic, minced
- 2 tablespoons butter or margarine
- 1 can (about 11 ounces) chicken gravy
- ⅓ cup water
- 2 tablespoons soy sauce
- ½ teaspoon salt
  Dash of pepper
- 3 cups diced roast pork
- 1 can (1 pound) bean sprouts, drained
- 1 can (5 ounces) water chestnuts, drained and sliced
- 1 nine-inch frozen pastry shell, thawed

1 Sauté onion, green pepper, celery and garlic in butter or margarine until soft in a large frying pan.
2 Stir in gravy, water, soy sauce, salt, pepper, pork, bean sprouts and water chestnuts; heat to boiling. Spoon into a deep 6-cup baking dish.
3 Spread pastry shell flat, then roll out, if needed, to a round 1 inch larger than baking

dish; cut several slits in center to let steam escape. Place over meat filling; fold overhang under, flush with rim; flute edge.

4 Bake in hot oven (400°) 30 minutes, or until pastry is golden.

Shanghai Pork
Makes 4 servings

Slice leftover roast ever so thin, then brush with its soy-seasoned baste and broil crispy-brown. Cut cold cooked pork shoulder butt into 8 to 12 thin slices; arrange in single layer on broiler rack. Brush with ⅓ cup orange juice blended with ⅓ cup each honey and soy sauce. Broil about 4 inches from heat, brushing often, 5 minutes on each side, or until very brown and crisp. Arrange slices in a ring on top of CHINESE VEGETABLE BOWL *(recipe follows)*; serve with buttered hot rice.

Chinese Vegetable Bowl
Do try this simple way to cook vegetables colorfully crisp.
Makes 4 to 6 servings

¼ cup peanut oil
1 Bermuda onion, sliced thin
2 cups thinly sliced celery
1 can (6 ounces) sliced mushrooms
1 package frozen Chinese pea pods
  OR: 1 package frozen Italian green beans
2 cups coarsely chopped Chinese cabbage
2 cups coarsely chopped escarole
1 can (5 ounces) water chestnuts, drained and
  sliced
  Soy sauce

1 Heat peanut oil in large frying pan; sauté onion lightly 2 to 3 minutes; add celery and liquid from mushrooms; cover; steam 5 minutes.
2 Lay Chinese pea pods or green beans, Chinese cabbage, escarole, water chestnuts and mushrooms in layers on top. Cover; steam 5 minutes longer, or just until crisply cooked.
3 Toss together, salad-bowl style; serve plain or with soy sauce.

Ham Soufflé
Bake at 350° for 45 minutes. Makes 6 servings

¼ cup (½ stick) butter or margarine
¼ cup sifted all-purpose flour
½ teaspoon dry mustard
¼ teaspoon salt
1 cup milk
¼ cup grated Parmesan cheese
1 cup ground cooked ham
6 eggs, separated

1 Melt butter or margarine in a medium-size saucepan; stir in flour, mustard and salt; cook, stirring constantly, just until bubbly. Stir in milk; continue cooking and stirring until sauce thickens and bubbles 1 minute.
2 Stir in cheese and ham; let cool while beating eggs.
3 Beat egg whites just until they form soft peaks in a large bowl. Beat egg yolks until creamy-thick in a second large bowl; blend in cooled sauce. Stir in about 1 cup of the beaten egg whites until blended, then fold in remainder until no streaks of white remain. Pour into an ungreased 8-cup soufflé or straight-side baking dish. Gently cut a deep circle in mixture about 1 inch from edge with a rubber spatula. (This gives soufflé its double-puff top.)
4 Bake in moderate oven (350°) 45 minutes, or until puffy-firm and golden on top. Serve at once.

Ham-and-Cheese Soufflé
Swiss cheese and ground ham make this delicately seasoned fancy.
Bake at 350° for 45 minutes. Makes 6 servings

3 tablespoons butter or margarine
3 tablespoons all-purpose flour
½ teaspoon dry mustard
¼ teaspoon salt
1 cup milk
1 cup shredded Swiss cheese (4 ounces)
½ teaspoon caraway seeds
1 cup ground baked ham
6 eggs, separated

1 Melt butter or margarine in a medium-size saucepan; stir in flour, mustard and salt; cook, stirring constantly, just until bubbly. Stir in milk; continue cooking and stirring until sauce thickens and boils 1 minute.
2 Stir in cheese until melted, caraway seeds and ham; let cool while beating eggs.
3 Beat egg whites just until they form soft peaks in a large bowl. Beat egg yolks until creamy-thick in a second large bowl; blend in cooled cheese sauce. Stir in about 1 cup of the beaten

egg whites until blended, then fold in remaining until no streaks of white remain. Pour into an ungreased 8-cup soufflé or straight-side baking dish. Gently cut a deep circle in mixture about 1 inch in from edge with a rubber spatula. (This gives soufflé its double-puffed top.)

4 Bake in moderate oven (350°) 45 minutes, or until puffy-firm and golden on top. Serve at once.

Curried Ham Soufflé

Here's an ideal way to use bits and pieces of cooked ham, as meat should be ground well. Bake at 350° for 1½ hours. Makes 6 servings

    4 tablespoons (½ stick) butter or margarine
    1 small onion, grated
    4 tablespoons all-purpose flour
    ½ teaspoon curry powder
    ¼ teaspoon salt
      Dash of pepper
    2 cups milk
    ½ cup soft bread crumbs (1 slice)
    2 cups ground cooked ham (about 1 pound)
    4 eggs

1 Melt butter or margarine in a large saucepan.

Blend in onion, flour, curry powder, salt and pepper; cook, stirring all the time, just until mixture bubbles.

2 Stir in milk; continue cooking and stirring until sauce thickens and boils 1 minute. Beat in bread crumbs until well blended; remove from heat; stir in ham.

3 Separate eggs, putting whites in a large bowl, yolks in a small bowl. Beat yolks slightly with a fork; blend in a few spoonfuls of the hot ham mixture, then quickly stir back into mixture in saucepan, blending well. Cool to lukewarm.

4 Beat egg whites until they form soft peaks; pour ham mixture over and gently fold in until no streaks of white remain.

5 Spoon into an ungreased 6-cup straight-side baking dish. Set dish in a shallow baking pan; place on oven shelf; pour boiling water into pan to a depth of 1 inch.

6 Bake in moderate oven (350°) 1½ hours, or until soufflé is puffy-light and firm in center. Serve at once.

Sherried Ham Tetrazzini

Three cups of ham cubes with creamy mushroom sauce make this popular main dish. Bake at 400° for 20 minutes. Makes 6 servings

From any leftover pork roast: Shanghai Pork, a soy-laced pinwheel crowning crisp Chinese Vegetable Bowl.

½ pound thin spaghetti
1 can (3 or 4 ounces) sliced mushrooms
1 medium-size onion, chopped (½ cup)
½ cup chopped celery
6 tablespoons (¾ stick) butter or margarine
6 tablespoons all-purpose flour
2 envelopes instant chicken broth
   OR: 2 chicken-bouillon cubes
¼ teaspoon pepper
1 cup cream
3 tablespoons dry sherry
3 cups cubed cooked ham
¼ cup grated Parmesan cheese

1 Break spaghetti in 2-inch pieces. Cook, following label directions; drain; place in a greased shallow 8-cup baking dish.
2 While spaghetti cooks, drain liquid from mushrooms into a 2-cup measure; add water to make 2 cups.
3 Sauté onion and celery in butter or margarine until soft in a large saucepan. Stir in flour, chicken broth or bouillon cubes and pepper. Cook, stirring constantly, until bubbly. Stir in the 2 cups liquid, cream and sherry. Continue cooking and stirring until sauce thickens and boils 1 minute; stir in mushrooms and ham.
4 Spoon over spaghetti in baking dish. Sprinkle with Parmesan cheese.
5 Bake in hot oven (400°) 20 minutes, or until bubbly.

Ham 'n' Eggplant Sandwiches
Makes 4 servings

1 large eggplant
4 slices cooked ham (about ¼ inch thick)
4 slices process Swiss cheese (from a 6-ounce package)
1 egg, beaten
   Water
½ teaspoon salt
1 cup fine dry bread crumbs
3 tablespoons vegetable oil

1 Cut 8 slices, ¼ inch thick, from eggplant. (Save remaining eggplant for another meal.) Pare eggplant slices; sandwich with ham and cheese slices.
2 Beat egg, 3 tablespoons water and salt in a pie plate. Spread crumbs on wax paper. Dip eggplant sandwiches first into egg mixture and then into crumbs to coat evenly.
3 Heat oil in a large skillet. Brown sandwiches on both sides in oil. Add ½ cup water to skillet; cover.
4 Cook 15 minutes, or until eggplant is tender.

1630

Saucy Ham and Asparagus Crêpes
Bake at 350° for 25 minutes. Makes 4 servings, 2 crepes each

CRÊPE BATTER (recipe follows)
1 package (10 ounces) frozen asparagus spears
3 tablespoons butter or margarine
2 tablespoons diced onion
3 tablespoons all-purpose flour
½ teaspoon salt
   Dash of cayenne
¾ cup milk
1 cup cream for whipping
1½ cups finely diced cooked ham
½ cup mayonnaise or salad dressing
   Paprika

1 Prepare CRÊPE BATTER; chill about 1 hour.
2 Heat a 7- to 8-inch skillet; lightly grease with butter or margarine; pour in ¼ cup batter; tip pan quickly to cover bottom completely.
3 Cook over medium heat until top appears dry and bottom is golden; turn; cook about ½ minute longer; turn out onto paper toweling. Repeat to make 8 crêpes, greasing pan between each.
4 Cook asparagus, following label directions; drain.
5 Melt butter or margarine in a medium-size saucepan; add onions; sauté 2 minutes. Stir in flour, salt, and cayenne; cook, stirring constantly, just until bubbly. Stir in milk and ¾ cup of the cream; continue cooking and stirring until sauce thickens and bubbles 1 minute. Measure out ¼ cup and save for topping. Stir ham into remaining sauce.
6 Fill crêpes: Place 2 or 3 asparagus spears on each crêpe; add about ¼ cup ham filling; roll up and place, seam side down in a buttered 13x9x2-inch baking dish.
7 Whip remaining ¼ cup cream; stir in saved cream sauce and mayonnaise or salad dressing. Spoon over filled crêpes; sprinkle with paprika.
8 Bake in moderate oven (350°) for 25 minutes, or until thoroughly heated.

CRÊPE BATTER—Beat 3 eggs in a medium-size bowl; stir in 1 cup milk; sift in 1 cup sifted all-purpose flour and ½ teaspoon salt; beat just until smooth; stir in 2 tablespoons vegetable oil; chill about 1 hour. Makes enough for 8 crêpes.

Country Ham Ring
Loaf in-the-round with mellow horseradish sauce for colorful contrast.
Bake at 350° for 1 hour. Makes 6 to 8 servings

1 small onion, chopped (¼ cup)
1 tablespoon butter or margarine
6 cups ground cooked ham (about 2 pounds)

2 cups soft white-bread crumbs (4 slices)
2 eggs, slightly beaten
½ cup buttermilk
2 tablespoons prepared mustard
   Dash of pepper
   HORSERADISH-CURRANT SAUCE (recipe follows)

1 Sauté onion in butter or margarine until soft in a small frying pan.
2 Combine with ham, bread crumbs, eggs, buttermilk, mustard and pepper in a large bowl; mix until well blended. Spoon into a 6-cup ring mold, packing down lightly with back of spoon.
3 Bake in moderate oven (350°) 1 hour, or until firm.
4 When ready to serve, loosen around edge and center with a knife; turn out onto a heated serving plate. Cut into wedges. Serve with HORSERADISH-CURRANT SAUCE.

HORSERADISH-CURRANT SAUCE—Melt 2 tablespoons butter or margarine in a small saucepan. Blend in 2 tablespoons all-purpose flour, then stir in ¾ cup water, ½ cup milk and 1 envelope instant chicken broth or 1 chicken-bouillon cube. Cook, stirring constantly, until sauce thickens and boils 1 minute. Stir in 2 tablespoons currants, 1 tablespoon sugar, 1 tablespoon cider vinegar and 2 teaspoons prepared horseradish. Serve warm. Makes about 1½ cups.

Country Ham and Potatoes
Enough ham left to dice? Turn it into this simple-fix, home-style dish.
Makes 4 servings

1 medium-size onion, chopped (½ cup)
4 tablespoons (½ stick) butter or margarine
2 cups diced baked ham
4 cups diced pared raw potatoes
2 tablespoons cream for whipping

1 Sauté onion in 2 tablespoons of the butter or margarine until soft in a large frying pan; remove and mix with ham in a medium-size bowl.
2 Place potatoes and remaining 2 tablespoons butter or margarine in same frying pan; cover. Cook slowly, without stirring, 20 minutes. Mash with a fork and shape into a large patty; spoon ham mixture in a layer on top, then press into potatoes; drizzle with cream. Cover again.
3 Cook slowly 25 minutes longer, or until a rich brown crust forms. Cut patty into quarters; lift onto heated serving plates.

Ham Divan
Sliced meat teams with broccoli and a tangy sauce for this second-day best.
Bake at 400° for 15 minutes. Makes 4 servings

1 package (10 ounces) frozen broccoli spears
4 slices white or French bread, toasted and buttered
4 large thin slices baked ham
1 cup (8-ounce carton) dairy sour cream
1 teaspoon prepared mustard
½ cup grated Cheddar cheese

1 Cook broccoli, following label directions; drain well.
2 Place toast slices in a single layer in a large shallow baking dish or in individual baking dishes; cover each with a slice of ham, folding ham, if needed, to fit toast; top with hot broccoli.
3 Blend sour cream with mustard in a small bowl; spoon in ribbons over broccoli; sprinkle with grated cheese.
4 Bake in hot oven (400°) 15 minutes, or until heated through and cheese melts.

Stuffed Ham Malaga
Slices of meat are folded over rice salad, then glazed with spicy orange sauce.
Bake at 350° for 30 minutes. Makes 6 servings

1 can (about 11 ounces) mandarin-orange segments
¼ cup orange marmalade
¼ teaspoon ground ginger
3 cups cooked rice
¼ cup chopped pecans
3 tablespoons sliced green onion
¼ cup mayonnaise or salad dressing
6 large thin slices baked ham

1 Drain liquid from mandarin-orange segments into a small saucepan; cook rapidly until reduced by half; stir in marmalade and ginger.
2 Set aside 12 mandarin-orange segments; mix remaining with remaining ingredients, except ham, in a bowl. Spoon about ⅔ cup onto each slice of ham; fold ham over to cover filling; place in a shallow baking dish, 10x6x2. Brush with part of the hot orange sauce.
3 Bake in moderate oven (350°), brushing with remaining orange sauce, 25 minutes; garnish with saved mandarin-orange segments; bake 5 minutes longer, or until hot.

1631

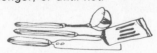

Ready for the salad bowl: America's lavish harvest of greens, tomatoes, peppers, avocados, apples and grapes.

**SALAD DAYS:
THE CARE AND KEEPING OF SALAD
GREENS, VEGETABLE SALADS, FRUIT
SALADS, MOLDED SALADS, MAIN
DISH SALADS, SALAD DRESSINGS**

Salads can comfortably serve as almost any course of a meal. Tart and crisp and served in small portions, they make splendid appetizers; frilly and green and lightly dressed, they accompany meat, fish or fowl to perfection; made *with* meat, fish or fowl, they themselves become savory, satisfying main dishes. Jellied or frozen and laden with fruit, they can double effectively as dessert, delighting the most finicky sweet tooth.

No other single category of food except, perhaps, for soup is more versatile. In the section that follows, you'll find a broad selection of salads: tossed green, cooked vegetable, fruit, main dish and molded salads. You'll also find a picture gallery of popular salad greens, tips for making perfect salads and a collection of classic salad dressings. The recipes, chosen from hundreds in the FAMILY CIRCLE files, represent the very best that the magazine has published down the years.

GREEN SALADS

THE CARE AND KEEPING
OF SALAD GREENS

When You Shop for Salad Greens:

The modern supermarket goes all out to attract salad buyers, with generous displays of varicolor greens on invitingly arranged counters. You will find crisp varieties sold by the head or pound, wrapped greens in transparent bags or on trays with see-through overwraps, packaged ready-to-use salad mixes, seasonal fresh herbs—dill, basil, mint—and many regional greens to make into an almost endless variety of tempting salads all year round.

In fact, there are so many kinds that you could serve a salad every day for two weeks and never repeat the same green. Often the prepackaged produce carries the brand name of your supermarket or the grower or distributor—another aid to quality buying, better sanitation and faster shopping.

How to Pick Top Quality Greens:

Pick out fairly firm, medium-size heads of lettuce, as larger ones may be overgrown and tend to be slightly bitter. If you spot a reddish discoloration at stem end, don't be concerned. This is nature's way of sealing the cut that was made when the head was picked and trimmed.

For variety and interest, look for the less familiar regional or seasonal greens. Just a few examples are: Prize head lettuce with red-edged leaves; lamb's lettuce; fennel, or finochio, with its distinctive anise flavor; the tender young dandelion, mustard and beet greens, plus Swiss chard. You can cook these greens, of course, but don't miss out on the unusual flavor touches

1633

that just a few, chopped up, will add to a salad bowl.

If any varieties are brand-new to you, don't hesitate to ask your produce man about them. As a general rule, you can count on about 4 servings from a medium-size head of iceberg lettuce, or 1 pound of loose greens, or a 1½-pound head of cabbage.

How to Care for and Store Greens:

Perfect salads start with perfect greens, and if you clean them and put them into the refrigerator fast, they should keep fresh and crisp for about a week.

Remove stems and any droopy leaves, then wash solid heads such as iceberg lettuce and cabbage and dry on paper toweling, or set on a wire rack or in a colander to drain. Swish leafy varieties such as Boston or leaf lettuce and curly endive up and down in a pan of lukewarm water, changing it, if needed. Warm water won't wilt the greens and helps to wash away every speck of soil or sand that much faster. Give greens a final rinsing in very cold water and drain well.

Store cleaned big heads in your vegetable crisper or large plastic bag, smaller varieties in individual bags.

Save the dark outer vitamin-rich leaves, unless they are badly bruised, to shred into a salad or put into sandwiches where appearance isn't so important. Some homemakers prefer to store delicate greens such as mint and watercress in small covered containers. All this takes time on shopping day, but pays off handsomely in family-good salads.

Salad-Making Tips:

Start with chilled, crackly-crisp greens. Use more than one variety—dark with light, mild with tangy—and tear, rather than cut, into bite-size pieces.

Choose your dressing carefully. A thin French dressing goes well with plain or mixed greens; a thicker French dressing or mayonnaise or salad dressing, with fruit, fish, vegetable or meat salad.

Keep the dressing simple, varying it with seasoning touches your family likes best. And be miserly, too, adding just enough dressing to coat the salad.

Use a light touch in tossing, reaching into the bottom of the bowl each time. Serve at once.

Classic Caesar Salad
Makes 6 servings

4 tablespoons olive oil

3 tablespoons wine vinegar or cider vinegar
2 tablespoons lemon juice
1 clove of garlic, minced
1 teaspoon salt
⅛ teaspoon coarsely ground pepper
1 large head of romaine
1 egg
¼ cup freshly grated Parmesan cheese
1 can anchovy fillets
1½ cups GOLDEN CROUTONS (recipe follows)

1 Combine olive oil, vinegar, lemon juice, garlic, salt and pepper in a large salad bowl.
2 Separate romaine leaves; wash and dry well. (This is important so that moisture does not dilute dressing). Cut out any coarse ribs; then break leaves in bite-size pieces into bowl. (You should have about 12 cups).
3 Place egg in boiling water in small saucepan; cover; remove from heat and let stand 1 minute to coddle. Remove from water at once.
4 Top greens with Parmesan cheese and anchovies (more or less to suit your taste, as they are salty); break coddled egg over all.
5 Toss salad, spooning from bottom of bowl each time, until greens are evenly coated with dressing. Sprinkle with GOLDEN CROUTONS; toss to coat well.

GOLDEN CROUTONS—Cut 3 slices slightly dry bread into small cubes; spread in a single layer in a shallow baking pan. Bake in a slow oven (300°) 15 minutes or until crisply golden. Makes 1½ cups.

Cool Cucumber Salad
One taste and we think you'll agree this way with cucumbers is most refreshing.
Makes 8 to 10 servings

3 medium-size cucumbers
3 teaspoons salt
1 cup (8-ounce container) plain yogurt
1 tablespoon vegetable oil
2 tablespoons chopped parsley
¼ teaspoon pepper
1 medium-size head of iceberg lettuce, broken into bite-size pieces (about 6 cups)

1 Pare cucumbers; slice thin (you should have about 4 cups). Mix with 2 teaspoons salt in medium-size bowl. (Save remaining teaspoon salt for Step 2.) Cover bowl; let stand 30 to 45 minutes. Pour into a strainer; let drain, then squeeze out as much liquid as possible.
2 Mix yogurt, vegetable oil, parsley, saved 1 teaspoon salt and pepper in same bowl; stir in well-drained cucumbers; chill until serving time.
3 Fill a large salad bowl with lettuce; pour cucumber dressing over; toss to coat greens well.

A GALLERY OF POPULAR SALAD GREENS

From chunky crisp iceberg lettuce to peppery watercress—here are the leaders of the salad-greens family. Use your favorite in your salad bowl, or mix them, for a contrast of two is good; three, even better.

Iceberg or Head Lettuce—*Big round compact head with light to dark green leaves. Everyday favorite.*

Boston or Butterhead Lettuce—*Soft loose head with tender delicately flavored green to light yellow leaves.*

Romaine or Cos Lettuce—*Long green crisp leaves with heavy ribs. Popular for mixed green-salad bowls.*

Bibb or Limestone Lettuce—*Tiny head of dark green leaves. Prized for its size, color, flavor, tenderness.*

Leaf or Garden Lettuce—*Ruffled pale green delicate leaves growing loosely from its small slender stalk.*

Green Cabbage—*Spring variety is bright green; late or winter, silvery green. An all-year winner for cole-slaw.*

Red or Purple Cabbage—*Easily recognized by color. Solid heavy head with a flavor stronger than the green.*

Savoy or Curly Cabbage—*Tightly crimped, heavily veined dark green leaves with a green-cabbage flavor.*

Chinese or Celery Cabbage—*Long oval compact head of pale green to white frilly leaves. Chop for salad.*

Belgian or French Endive—*Tiny tight sticklike head of cream-white leaves. A European-grown specialty.*

Chicory or Curly Endive—*Floppy head with feathery dark to very pale green leaves. Pleasingly bitter flavor.*

Escarole—*Cross between lettuce and chicory with broad curly leaves and yellowish center. Slightly bitter.*

Spinach—*Dark green flat crinkly leaves with coarse stems. For salad, use tender leaves with stems removed.*

Watercress—*Little shiny dark green leaves branching out from a slender stalk. Tastes bitey, pungent.*

Green-and-Gold Salad

Bright avocado and sunny oranges make this salad refreshingly springlike.
Makes 6 servings

1 small head of iceberg lettuce
1 medium-size ripe avocado, peeled and sliced
3 oranges, peeled and sectioned
1 small onion, sliced thin and separated into rings
CELERY-SEED DRESSING *(recipe follows)*

1 Line 6 small salad bowls with lettuce leaves; break remaining into bite-size pieces, dividing evenly among bowls.
2 Arrange avocado slices, orange sections and onion rings on top.
3 Drizzle each with about 1 tablespoon CELERY-SEED DRESSING. Pass extra dressing, if you like.
   CELERY-SEED DRESSING—Combine 1 teaspoon grated onion, ½ teaspoon salt, ½ teaspoon dry mustard, ½ teaspoon paprika, ½ teaspoon celery seeds, ½ cup vegetable oil, ¼ cup light corn syrup and 3 tablespoons cider vinegar in jar with tight-fitting cover. Shake until well blended. Keep covered in refrigerator. Shake again just before using. Makes about 1 cup.

Continental Green Salad

Crushed coriander seeds give this simple salad a refreshingly different flavor.
Makes 6 to 8 servings

8 cups broken mixed salad greens (romaine, leaf and iceberg lettuce)
1 small yellow squash, sliced thin
1 small sweet red pepper, seeded and sliced into thin rings
1 small red onion, sliced thin and separated into rings
¼ pound sharp Cheddar cheese, cubed
½ cup olive oil or vegetable oil
¼ cup wine vinegar or cider vinegar
   Coriander seeds, crushed
   Salt and pepper

1 Fill a large salad bowl with greens, squash slices, red-pepper and onion rings and cheese cubes; toss lightly. (This can be done ahead. Then slide bowl into a large transparent plastic bag, or cover with foil or transparent wrap, and place in the refrigerator to keep chilled until serving time.)

2 Serve salad in individual bowls for each to dress his own with oil and vinegar, mixed; a tiny sprinkling of crushed coriander seeds; and salt and pepper.
Note—If you have any greens left over, wrap loosely in transparent wrap or foil and save for a next-day's meal, they'll keep freshly crisp if they have no dressing on them.

Tart Spinach Salad

It's a hot salad specialty of a famous Hollywood restaurant. Try it—it's deliciously different.
Makes 8 servings

½ pound fresh spinach
6 slices (from a 6-ounce package) Italian assortment cold cuts, diced
⅓ cup vegetable oil
¼ cup cider vinegar
1 teaspoon sugar
½ teaspoon seasoned salt
2 teaspoons soy sauce
1 teaspoon prepared mustard

1 Remove stems and any large ribs from spinach; wash leaves; drain well, then tear into bite-size pieces. (You should have about 12 cups.) Place in large salad bowl.
2 Sauté diced cold cuts in vegetable oil just until heated through in medium-size frying pan. Stir in remaining ingredients; heat, stirring constantly, just to boiling.
3 Pour at once over spinach; toss to coat all leaves well. Serve immediately.

Green Salad with Grapes and Walnuts

Serve fruit and cheese the salad way! Orange dressing is refreshingly tart and pleasing.
Makes 6 servings

4 heads Bibb lettuce
1 cup cubed Swiss cheese
1 firm ripe peach, halved, pitted and sliced
1 can (about 9 ounces) pineapple tidbits, drained
½ cup purple grapes, halved and seeded
¼ cup walnut halves
   GINGER ORANGE DRESSING *(recipe follows)*

1 Cut core from each head of lettuce and separate into leaves; wash well; dry thoroughly. Place in a large salad bowl with cheese, peach slices, pineapple, grapes and walnuts.
2 Drizzle part of the GINGER ORANGE DRESSING on top; toss lightly to mix. Serve with remaining dressing.
   GINGER ORANGE DRESSING—Combine ¼ cup

Nuts, fruit and lettuce team in Green Salad with Grapes and Walnuts. Ginger Orange Dressing adds zip.

vegetable oil, 2 tablespoons thawed frozen concentrated orange juice (from a 6-ounce can), 1 tablespoon honey, ¼ teaspoon salt and ⅛ teaspoon ground ginger in a small jar with a tight-fitting lid; shake well to mix. Makes about ½ cup.

Summer's Best Green Salad
Peak-of-the-season greens and green onions, tossed with a low-calorie tomato dressing, make this a family favorite.
Makes 6 servings

1 small head of romaine
1 small head of leaf lettuce
3 green onions, sliced
1 envelope French salad-dressing mix
¾ cup fresh or canned tomato juice
¼ cup cider vinegar
2 tablespoons water

1 Break romaine and lettuce leaves into bite-size pieces in a large bowl. (There should be about 6 cups.) Add onions.
2 Combine salad-dressing mix, tomato juice, vinegar and water in a jar with tight-fitting lid; shake well to mix.
3 Drizzle about ¼ cup over greens; toss to coat well. Pass remaining dressing, if you wish.

White Mountain Radish Bowl
Lots of tangy radishes are seasoned with a sweet-sour dressing for this delightful variation on tossed salad.
Makes 6 servings

6 cups broken escarole or lettuce
4 bunches radishes, trimmed and sliced thin (about 4 cups)
8 slices bacon, diced
2 tablespoons sugar
2 tablespoons wine vinegar or cider vinegar
2 tablespoons water
1 teaspoon seasoned salt

1 Place escarole or lettuce in a large salad bowl; mound sliced radishes on top.
2 Sauté bacon until crisp in a medium-size frying pan; remove and drain on paper toweling.
3 Pour drippings into a cup, then measure 4 tablespoonfuls back into pan; stir in sugar, wine vinegar or cider vinegar, water and seasoned salt. Heat to boiling; remove from heat.
4 Pour over radishes in bowl; add bacon; toss lightly to mix.

1637

Parsley Chiffonade Salad
Crisp green parsley gives this salad a pungent flavor that men especially like.
Makes 6 servings

1 large bunch of parsley
4 hard-cooked eggs, coarsely chopped
3 medium-size tomatoes, peeled and diced

1 can (4 ounces) sardines, drained and cut up
VEGETABLE DRESSING (recipe follows)

1 Wash parsley, remove stems, and dry well on paper toweling (you should have about 6 cups). Place in large salad bowl; sprinkle eggs, tomatoes and sardines over.
2 Pour VEGETABLE DRESSING over parsley mixture, tossing to coat salad well.

Vegetable Dressing
Makes ⅓ cup

¼ cup olive oil or vegetable oil
2 tablespoons wine vinegar or cider vinegar
6 radishes, grated
½ clove of garlic, minced
½ teaspoon sugar
½ teaspoon paprika
⅛ teaspoon pepper

Combine all ingredients in small jar with tight-fitting cover; shake well just before serving.

VEGETABLE SALADS

Old-Fashioned Cabbage Slaw
Thinly sliced apple and a little fennel seed highlight cabbage salad.
Makes 8 servings

1 head cabbage (about 2½ pounds)
½ cup sugar
3 teaspoons salt
1 teaspoon fennel seeds, crushed
2 medium-size tart red apples
2 tablespoons lemon juice
1 cup mayonnaise or salad dressing
½ cup dairy sour cream

1 Trim cabbage; quarter; shred fine. (You will have about 10 cups.) Combine with sugar, salt and fennel seed in a large salad bowl; toss to mix well; let stand at room temperature, tossing occasionally, about ½ hour; drain, discarding liquid.
2 Meanwhile, quarter and core apples (do not pare); cut into very thin slices; toss with lemon juice in a small bowl.
3 Just before serving, blend mayonnaise or salad dressing and sour cream in a small bowl. Toss apples with drained cabbage; pour dressing over cabbage mixture; toss until evenly coated.

Chinese Slaw
Toss refreshing oranges and crisp Chinese cabbage with a ginger-flavored dressing.
Makes 8 servings

8 cups shredded Chinese cabbage (1 small head)
4 large oranges
2 tablespoons cut chives
¾ cup mayonnaise or salad dressing
2 tablespoons sugar
½ teaspoon ground ginger
2 tablespoons lemon juice

1 Place cabbage in a large salad bowl; pare and section oranges over a small bowl to catch juice; reserve. Pile orange sections in center of cabbage; sprinkle chives over all.
2 Blend mayonnaise or salad dressing, sugar, ginger, lemon juice and 2 tablespoons of the reserved orange juice in a small bowl.
3 Just before serving, pour dressing over salad; toss lightly until evenly coated.

Farmer's Slaw
Marinated shredded yellow turnip and mellow pears are a surprise salad combo.
Makes 8 servings

⅔ cup vegetable oil
⅓ cup cider vinegar
3 tablespoons sugar
1 teaspoon salt
¼ teaspoon ground mace
¼ teaspoon dry mustard
¼ teaspoon paprika
4 cups shredded yellow turnip (1 small turnip, about 1½ pounds)
2 large fresh pears
2 teaspoons lemon juice
6 cups finely cut romaine

1 Combine oil, vinegar, sugar, salt, mace, mustard and paprika in a jar with a tight lid; shake well to mix; pour dressing over turnip in a medium-size bowl; cover; chill 1 hour to season.
2 Pare pears; quarter, core and dice. Toss with lemon juice in a small bowl; cover; chill until ready to serve.
3 Just before serving, place romaine in a large salad bowl; arrange turnip and dressing around edge; spoon pears in center; toss until evenly coated.

Triple Vegetable Slaw
Pungent yellow turnip and sweet red beet give color and zing to this winter salad.
Makes 6 servings

4 cups finely shredded cabbage
6 tablespoons NO-COOK "BOILED" DRESSING (recipe follows)
2 cups shredded pared yellow turnip
1 small red apple, quartered, cored and chopped
½ cup shredded pared beet

1 Toss cabbage with 3 tablespoons of the dressing in a medium-size bowl. Toss turnip and apple with remaining 3 tablespoons dressing in a second medium size bowl.
2 Spoon cabbage mixture into a salad bowl; mound turnip-apple mixture on top. Garnish with a cone of shredded beet.

No-Cook "Boiled" Dressing
Its flavor is just sweet and tart enough. And it keeps perfectly in the refrigerator.
Makes about 2½ cups

1 egg
1 tablespoon dry mustard
1 teaspoon salt
½ teaspoon paprika
Dash of cayenne
1 cup cider vinegar

1 can (14 or 15 ounces) sweetened condensed milk
4 tablespoons (½ stick) butter or margarine, melted

1 Beat egg until thick in a medium-size bowl. Beat in mustard, salt, paprika and cayenne; slowly beat in vinegar.
2 Stir in condensed (*not evaporated*) milk and melted butter or margarine; beat again until well blended.
3 Store leftover dressing in a covered jar in the refrigerator.

Tomato Fan-Tans
Cucumbers in sour cream make both the filling and the dressing for this salad with a different twist.
Makes 6 servings

½ cup dairy sour cream
1 teaspoon sugar
1 teaspoon salt
Dash of pepper
1 teaspoon prepared horseradish
2 tablespoons lemon juice
1 medium-size cucumber, sliced thin

A salad is only as good as what goes into it. Greens should be crinkly-fresh, vegetables plump and ripe.

1 small onion, sliced and separated into rings
6 medium-size tomatoes, peeled
Lettuce

1 Blend sour cream, sugar, salt, pepper, horse-radish and lemon juice in a 1-cup measure. Pour over cucumber and onion slices in a small bowl; toss to mix; cover. Chill at least an hour to season and blend flavors.
2 Place tomatoes, stem end down, on cutting board; make 5 parallel cuts almost to bottom in each; spread apart slightly.
3 Place tomatoes on lettuce-lined salad plates; spoon the cucumber mixture into cuts.

Tomatoes Lutèce, sandwiched with minced parsley.

Tomatoes Lutèce
Juicy tomatoes, sliced and stacked into shape again, are marinated in a Parisian dressing.
Makes 8 servings

8 firm ripe tomatoes, peeled
¼ cup chopped parsley
1 clove of garlic, crushed
1 teaspoon salt
1 teaspoon sugar
¼ teaspoon pepper
¼ cup olive oil or vegetable oil
2 tablespoons tarragon vinegar or cider vinegar
2 teaspoons prepared mustard

1 Cut out stem ends from tomatoes; slice each tomato crosswise into ½-inch-thick slices; re-form into tomato shape again and place in shallow serving dish.
2 Combine remaining ingredients in small jar; cover; shake well; pour over tomatoes.
3 Cover lightly; let stand at room temperature at least 20 minutes before serving. (Any left over? Chill and serve the next day.)

1640

Relish Tomatoes
So simple to fix, yet so tempting! Celery gives the dressing a pleasing crunch.
Makes 8 servings

8 medium-size tomatoes, peeled
½ cup finely chopped parsley
½ cup finely chopped celery
1 small onion, finely chopped (¼ cup)
1 tablespoon sugar
1 teaspoon seasoned salt
½ teaspoon seasoned pepper
¼ teaspoon thyme
¼ teaspoon curry powder

1 cup olive oil or vegetable oil
⅓ cup wine vinegar or cider vinegar

1 Cut out stem ends of tomatoes; cut tomatoes into ½-inch-thick slices; arrange in layers in a large shallow serving bowl.
2 Combine remaining ingredients in a jar with tight-fitting lid; shake well to mix; pour over tomatoes; cover. Chill at least an hour to season and blend flavors. (Save any remaining dressing in bowl for tossing with green salad for another meal.)

Tomato Bouquet Salad
How pretty it looks with a nosegay of vegetables centering a ring of herb-seasoned tomatoes.
Makes 8 servings

4 large ripe tomatoes, peeled and sliced ½ inch thick
1 tablespoon sugar
1 teaspoon salt
1 teaspoon leaf basil, crumbled
Dash of pepper
½ small head curly endive, washed, dried and separated in leaves
1 small carrot, pared and cut in 3-inch-long thin sticks
1 small stalk celery, trimmed and cut in 3-inch-long thin sticks
4 pitted ripe olives
½ cup mayonnaise or salad dressing
2 tablespoons light cream or table cream
1 tablespoon lemon juice

1 Place tomato slices in a single layer in a

shallow dish. Mix sugar, salt, basil and pepper in a cup; sprinkle over tomatoes; cover; chill until serving time.

2 When ready to serve, arrange tomato slices, overlapping, around edge of a shallow serving bowl; fill center with a "nest" of endive; tuck carrot and celery sticks into endive. Thread olives onto a kebab stick; place in center of salad.

3 Blend mayonnaise or salad dressing, cream and lemon juice in a small bowl.

4 Pass dressing separately to spoon over salad.

●

Tomato-Cucumber Cups
Jumbo tomatoes are hollowed out and filled brimful with tangy cucumber slices.
Makes 6 servings

2 medium-size cucumbers
1 tablespoon finely cut fresh dill
3 tablespoons sugar
¼ teaspoon salt
⅛ teaspoon pepper
½ cup cider vinegar
6 large firm ripe tomatoes

1 Score cucumbers with a fork, then slice thin; set aside 6 slices for garnish. Place remaining in a medium-size bowl.

2 Combine dill, sugar, salt, pepper and vinegar in a cup; stir until sugar dissolves, then pour over cucumbers; toss lightly to mix; chill.

3 Cut a thin slice from bottom of each tomato; scoop out insides with a teaspoon. (Save pulp to add to soup.) Turn tomato cups upside down on paper toweling to drain. Chill cups and slices.

4 Just before serving, drain cucumbers; spoon into tomato cups; replace tops. Garnish each with a saved cucumber slice, a sprig of fresh dill and a radish threaded onto a wooden pick, if you wish. (To fix radishes, trim stem and root ends. Make about 6 cuts lengthwise into each, then make another cut just behind each line and lift out a narrow strip of peel.)

●

Tomato-Shrimp Cups
Scooped-out tomatoes, heaped with "green" rice and shrimp salad, make this dish.
Makes 4 servings

4 large tomatoes
Seasoned salt
1 cup uncooked regular rice
4 tablespoons thin French dressing
1 pound frozen, deveined, shelled, raw shrimps
1 small onion, sliced

½ lemon, sliced
½ cup water
½ cup diced cucumber
½ cup diced green pepper
2 tablespoons chopped parsley
2 tablespoons chopped fresh dill
1 tablespoon chopped chives
½ teaspoon salt
½ cup mayonnaise or salad dressing

1 Cut off tops of tomatoes; scoop out insides with a teaspoon. (Save pulp for making stewed tomatoes or soup.) Sprinkle shells lightly with seasoned salt; turn upside down on plate to drain, then chill while making rice-shrimp filling.

2 Cook rice, following label directions; drain; spoon into a medium-size bowl. Drizzle 2 tablespoons of the French dressing over; toss lightly; cover. Let stand at room temperature while cooking and seasoning shrimps. (Save remaining French dressing for Step 4.)

3 Combine shrimps, onion, lemon and water in a large frying pan; cover; simmer 20 minutes, or until shrimps are tender. Lift out with a slotted spoon; place in a medium-size bowl.

4 When cool enough to handle, set 4 large shrimps aside for topping cups in Step 6; halve remaining. Drizzle saved 2 tablespoons French dressing over; toss to mix well; cover. Chill at least an hour to season and blend flavors.

5 Just before serving, stir shrimps, cucumber, green pepper, parsley, dill, chives and salt into rice; fold in mayonnaise or salad dressing until well blended.

Tomato-Cucumber Cups make colorful luncheon fare.

1641

Calico Cups are made with canned tomatoes and corn.

6 Pile into tomato cups; garnish each with a saved whole shrimp and an additional cucumber slice, held in place with a wooden pick.

Calico Cups
Zippy Mexican-style corn fills hollowed-out canned tomatoes for this winter special.
Makes 6 servings

2 cans (1 pound each) peeled whole tomatoes
1 can (12 ounces) Mexican-style corn
½ cup bottled oil-and-vinegar salad dressing
2 teaspoons grated onion
    Bibb lettuce

1 Empty tomatoes carefully into a large shallow pan. (There should be 3 in each can.) Lift out, one at a time, with a slotted spoon and drain on paper toweling, then gently scoop out insides. (Chill pulp and juice to add to soup or stew.) Set tomato cups in a pie plate.
2 Heat corn just to boiling in a small saucepan; drain. Stir in oil-and-vinegar dressing and onion; spoon into tomato cups; cover. Chill at least two hours to season and blend flavors.
3 When ready to serve, place each tomato on a lettuce-lined salad plate; top each with a sprig of parsley and serve with a dollop of your favorite mayonnaise or salad dressing, if you wish.

Triple Vegetable Bowl
Layers of seasoned yellow squash, tomatoes and limas make this gay, colorful salad.
Makes 8 servings

2 pounds lima beans, shelled (2 cups)
    OR: 1 package (10 ounces) frozen baby lima beans
4 small yellow squashes
5 medium-size tomatoes
1 cherry tomato, peeled
1 envelope Parmesan salad-dressing mix
    Cider vinegar
    Vegetable oil
2 tablespoons chopped parsley

1 Cook lima beans, covered, in boiling salted water in medium-size saucepan 25 minutes, or until tender; drain. Place in a shallow dish. (Or cook the frozen lima beans, following label directions.)
2 Trim squashes; cut into thin slices. Cook, covered, in small amount boiling salted water in medium-size saucepan 15 minutes, or until crisply tender; drain well. Place in a second shallow dish.
3 Peel tomatoes and cut out stem ends; cut each into ¼-inch-thick slices. Re-form 1 into its tomato shape, then place slices, "whole" tomato and cherry tomato in a third shallow dish.
4 Prepare salad-dressing mix with vinegar, water and vegetable oil, following label directions; add parsley and shake to mix well. Pour over vegetables, dividing evenly among dishes; cover. Chill at least an hour to season and blend flavors.
5 When ready to serve, spoon squash, then tomato slices, then lima beans into a shallow serving bowl; place "whole" tomato on top. Place cherry tomato on wooden pick; stick on top of large one. Garnish with a sprig of fresh dill, if you wish.

Winter Beet Salad
Makes 4 to 6 servings

1 envelope onion-flavor salad dressing mix
    Cider vinegar
    Vegetable oil
1 can (1 pound) julienne beets, drained
4 cups shredded iceberg lettuce
2 hard-cooked eggs, shelled and diced
¼ cup sliced pimiento-stuffed olives
¼ cup mayonnaise or salad dressing

1 Prepare salad dressing mix with vinegar, water and vegetable oil, following label directions. Measure out ¼ cupful and drizzle over beets in a small bowl; toss lightly. Let stand at least an hour to season. (Chill remaining dressing to use another day.)
2 Place lettuce in a large salad bowl. Drain dressing from beets into a small bowl; spoon beets in a ring around edge on lettuce. Spoon

eggs in a ring next to beets; pile olives in center.
3 Beat mayonnaise or salad dressing into onion dressing in bowl; drizzle over salad. Toss lightly to mix.

Winter Supper Salad Bowl
Makes 6 servings

1 can (about 1 pound) cut green beans
1 can (about 1 pound) lima beans
1 can (about 1 pound) cut wax beans
1 can (about 1 pound) red kidney beans
1 can (about 1 pound) chick peas
  Bottled thin French dressing
1 package (8 ounces) sliced process Swiss,
  American or brick cheese
1 package (6 ounces) round bologna
6 cups broken salad greens
1 hard-cooked egg, shelled and sieved·
2 tablespoons grated raw carrot
¼ teaspoon dillweed
1 small onion, peeled, sliced thin and separated into rings
1 tablespoon pickle relish

1 Drain liquid from all of the canned beans and chick peas; place each vegetable in a separate small bowl. Spoon 2 tablespoons French dressing over each; toss to mix, then set aside while fixing rest of salad.
2 Place cheese and bologna slices in stacks of 4 or 5 layers each; cut each stack into quarters to make triangular ''sandwiches.''
3 Place salad greens in a large salad bowl; pile seasoned vegetables in separate mounds on top. Sprinkle green beans with sieved egg, limas with grated carrot, wax beans with dillweed, kidney beans with sliced onion and chick peas with pickle relish. Tuck meat-and-cheese ''sandwiches'' around edge. Toss salad at table, adding more French dressing, if you wish.

Bouquet Vegetable Salad
Serve this summer-garden medley with cold sliced roast beef or hotdogs.
Makes 6 servings

3 medium-size beets
3 medium-size carrots
3 medium-size potatoes
2 cups thinly sliced celery
1 can (3 or 4 ounces) mushroom caps, drained
3 tablespoons bottled Italian salad dressing

Canned Vegetable combo: Western Pea Salad.

8 cups broken mixed salad greens
  CAPER CREAM DRESSING (recipe follows)

1 Trim tops of beets, leaving a 2-inch stem. Pare carrots and slice thin. Pare potatoes; cut into 1-inch cubes.
2 Cook beets in boiling salted water in a medium-size saucepan 20 minutes, or until tender; drain. Cut off stems and root ends and slip off skins; cut beets into ½-inch cubes; place in a small bowl.
3 Cook carrots and potatoes in boiling salted water in separate medium-size saucepans 10 minutes, or until tender; drain.
4 Place carrots, potatoes, celery and mushrooms in separate mounds in a large shallow dish. Spoon 1 tablespoon of the Italian dressing over beets and remaining over other vegetables. Chill all at least an hour to season and blend flavors.
5 When ready to serve, place salad greens in a large shallow bowl; arrange each vegetable, spoke fashion, on top. Spoon CAPER CREAM DRESSING over; toss lightly to mix.
  CAPER CREAM DRESSING—Blend 1 cup mayonnaise or salad dressing with 2 tablespoons bottled chili sauce, 2 tablespoons chopped sweet pickle and 1 tablespoon capers in a small bowl; chill. Makes about 1¼ cups.

Western Pea Salad
For this delightfully different salad, combine chick and green peas with crisp lettuce and zippy Italian dressing.
Makes 6 servings

1643

1 can (1 pound, 4 ounces) chick peas
1 can (1 pound) green peas
½ cup sliced green onions
1 envelope Italian salad-dressing mix
    Vegetable oil
    Cider vinegar
1 medium-size head iceberg lettuce
1 cup sliced celery
1½ cups pitted ripe olives, halved

1 Heat chick peas and green peas almost to boiling in separate small saucepans; drain. Spoon in two piles in a large shallow dish; sprinkle both vegetables evenly with the green onions.
2 Prepare Italian salad-dressing mix with vegetable oil, vinegar and water, following label directions. Drizzle ⅓ cup over vegetables; toss each lightly to mix; cover. Chill at least two hours to season and blend flavors. (Set remaining dressing aside for Step 4.)
3 When ready to serve, break lettuce into bite-size pieces in a large salad bowl; spoon chick peas in center and green peas around edge. Tuck celery slices around chick peas and arrange olive halves around edge of bowl.
4 Garnish with green-onion ruffles, if you wish, and serve with additional dressing. (To make green-onion ruffles: Trim 2 or 3 small green onions, then shred tops of each with a knife. Place in a bowl of ice and water until tops curl. Drain well and pat dry with a sheet of paper toweling before arranging in salad bowl.)

Bean-and-Bacon Salad
Generous amount of crisp bacon tops kidney beans and greens in a tart dressing.
Makes 6 servings

2 cans (1 pound, 4 ounces each) white kidney beans, well drained
    OR: 2 cans (1 pound each) red kidney beans, well drained
1 cup diced sweet green pepper
1 cup diced celery
½ cup thinly sliced green onions
1 pound bacon
1 large head iceberg lettuce
    TANGY TOMATO DRESSING (recipe follows)

1 Combine beans with green pepper, celery and onions in a medium-size bowl; chill.
2 Cut bacon into 1-inch pieces, sauté until crisp in a medium-size frying pan; drain well on paper toweling.
3 Break lettuce into bite-size pieces; divide among 6 soup plates or shallow salad bowls; spoon bean mixture over each; top with bacon.
4 Drizzle each with TANGY TOMATO DRESSING;

1644

toss lightly to mix. Garnish with watercress, if you wish.
    TANGY TOMATO DRESSING—Drain juice from 1 can (1 pound) tomatoes and save for soup. Press tomatoes through a fine sieve into a small bowl. Beat in ¼ cup mayonnaise or salad dressing; 1 clove garlic, crushed; 1 teaspoon sugar; 1 teaspoon salt; ½ teaspoon crumbled leaf marjoram; ⅛ teaspoon pepper; and 1 tablespoon lemon juice. Makes about 1¼ cups.

Mexicali Salad Ring
What a refreshing combination of red beans, mandarin oranges and sweet onion!
Makes 4 to 6 servings

1 can (about 1 pound) red kidney beans
1 can (11 ounces) mandarin-orange segments
½ cup coarsely chopped sweet onion
¼ cup chopped parsley
¼ cup vegetable oil
2 tablespoons cider vinegar
1 teaspoon sugar
½ teaspoon salt
    Lettuce

1 Drain kidney beans and mandarin-orange segments. Toss onion with parsley in a small bowl; mix vegetable oil, vinegar, sugar and salt in a cup.
2 Line a shallow serving bowl with lettuce. Spoon beans in a ring around edge and mandarin-orange segments next to beans; pile onion mixture in center. Drizzle dressing over; toss lightly.

Ruffled Squash Boats
Seasoned zucchini slices and red kidney beans sail to the table in scooped-out yellow-squash halves.
Makes 6 servings

3 large yellow squashes, trimmed and halved lengthwise
4 small zucchini, trimmed and sliced ¼ inch thick
1 can (about 1 pound) red kidney beans, drained
¾ cup bottled Italian salad dressing
2 tablespoons chopped parsley
    Lettuce

1 Cook yellow-squash halves in boiling salted water in a large frying pan 12 minutes, or until crisply tender; lift out with a slotted spoon. Carefully scoop out center of each; turn shells upside down on paper toweling to drain. Place in a single layer in a shallow dish.

Crisp coleslaw fills jaunty Calico Pepper Baskets.

Ruffled Squash Boats, zippy mix of squash and beans.

2 Cook zucchini in boiling salted water in a medium-size saucepan 8 minutes, or until crisply tender; drain. Place in a pie plate. Place kidney beans in a second pie plate.

3 Mix salad dressing and parsley in a 1-cup measure; drizzle ¼ cup over each of the squashes and beans; cover. Chill at least an hour to season and blend flavors.

4 When ready to serve, arrange zucchini slices, overlapping, in yellow-squash halves on lettuce-lined salad plates; spoon kidney beans in center. Garnish with sprigs of parsley, if you wish.

Calico Pepper Baskets
A simple cutting trick turns green and red peppers into pretty "dishes" for crisp coleslaw.
Makes 6 servings

    8 cups finely shredded cabbage (about 2
       pounds)
    2 tablespoons sugar
    3 medium-size sweet red peppers
    3 medium-size green peppers
    ½ cup shredded carrot
    2 tablespoons mayonnaise or salad dressing
    2 tablespoons lemon juice
    2 tablespoons light cream or table cream
    ¼ teaspoon salt
    ⅛ teaspoon pepper
       Lettuce

1 Place cabbage in a large bowl; sprinkle with sugar; toss lightly to mix; cover. Chill at least 30 minutes to crisp and mellow cabbage.

2 Make pepper baskets this way: Holding each pepper stem end down, mark a guideline around center with wooden picks. Then mark a ½-inch-wide strip across top for basket handle. Cut out sections between marks. Scoop out seeds and membrane; chill peppers. Chop cut pieces fine for next step.

3 Just before serving, drain cabbage. Add carrot and ¼ cup of the chopped green pepper and 1 tablespoon of the chopped red pepper.

4 Blend mayonnaise or salad dressing, lemon juice, cream, salt and pepper in a cup; pour over cabbage; toss to coat cabbage evenly.

5 Spoon into pepper baskets; place on lettuce-lined salad plates. Garnish each basket with a carrot curl, if you wish. (To make, shave long thin strips from a pared carrot with a vegetable parer. Wind each around fingertip; fasten with a wooden pick. Place in a bowl of ice and water until they're curled and crisp.)

Oriental Toss
Popular foods of the Far East are layered into a bowl, then topped with a curry-sparked dressing.
Makes 8 servings

    2 cans (1 pound each) bean sprouts, drained
    ¼ cup thin French dressing
    1 teaspoon soy sauce
    2 cups broken fresh spinach
    1 small green pepper, stemmed, seeded and
       cut in thin rings
    1 can (about 1 pound, 5 ounces) pineapple
       chunks
    1 can (5 ounces) water chestnuts, drained and
       sliced
    ¼ cup chopped peanuts
       CURRY DRESSING (recipe follows)

1 Place bean sprouts in a medium-size bowl; drizzle with French dressing and soy sauce; toss to mix; cover. Chill, tossing several times, at least an hour to season and blend flavors.

1645

2 Just before serving, place spinach in a large shallow salad bowl. Drain bean sprouts; layer with green-pepper rings over spinach in bowl.
3 Drain syrup from pineapple chunks into a cup; layer fruit and water chestnuts over green pepper. Sprinkle with peanuts.
4 Spoon CURRY DRESSING over all; toss lightly with two forks until well coated.

CURRY DRESSING—Blend ½ cup mayonnaise or salad dressing, 2 tablespoons of the saved pineapple syrup and ¼ teaspoon curry powder until smooth in a small bowl; chill. Makes about ½ cup.

Sun-Gold Potato Mold
This party-size classic, molded prettily in an angel-cake pan, looks so inviting with its bright egg topper.
Makes 12 to 16 servings

15 medium-size potatoes
⅓ cup vegetable oil
3 tablespoons cider vinegar
1 tablespoon grated onion
2 teaspoons salt
1 teaspoon leaf basil, crumbled
1 teaspoon dry mustard
⅛ teaspoon pepper
6 hard-cooked eggs, shelled
1 cup chopped green pepper
1 cup chopped sweet red pepper
1 cup chopped celery
1 cup mayonnaise or salad dressing
¼ cup milk

1 Cook potatoes in boiling salted water in a large saucepan 45 minutes, or just until tender; drain. Peel while still warm; cut into small cubes; place in a very large bowl. (There should be about 12 cups.)
2 Combine vegetable oil, vinegar, onion, salt, basil, mustard and pepper in a 1-cup measure; pour over potatoes; toss lightly until dressing is absorbed.
3 Halve 2 eggs; remove yolks and set aside in a cup for Step 6. Chop egg whites and remaining 4 eggs; add to potatoes with green pepper, red pepper and celery.
4 Blend mayonnaise or salad dressing and milk in a small bowl; fold into potato mixture.
5 Spoon into a 10-inch tube pan; press down lightly with back of spoon to make top even; cover. Chill several hours to season and blend flavors.
6 When ready to serve, loosen salad around edge and tube of pan with a thin-blade knife; invert pan over serving plate; let salad slide out; lift off pan. Press saved egg yolks through a

1646

sieve onto top of salad. Garnish with tiny sprigs of parsley, if you wish.

German Potato Salad Bowls
Smoky bacon tops this mellow potato salad that's served warm.
Makes 6 servings

6 cups diced pared potatoes (about 6 medium-size)
1 cup diced celery
½ cup diced sour pickles
1 medium-size onion, chopped (½ cup)
12 slices bacon, halved
2 tablespoons brown sugar
½ teaspoon salt
¼ teaspoon pepper
2 tablespoons cider vinegar
2 tablespoons water

1 Cook potatoes in boiling salted water in a large saucepan 10 minutes, or just until tender; drain, then shake pan gently over low heat to dry potatoes. Stir in celery, pickles and onion; cover; keep warm.
2 Sauté bacon until crisp in a medium-size frying pan; remove and drain on paper toweling. Crumble 12 pieces and add to potato mixture; set remaining pieces aside for garnish in Step 4.
3 Pour off all drippings from frying pan into a cup, then measure 2 tablespoons back into pan. Stir in brown sugar, salt, pepper, vinegar and water; heat, stirring constantly, to boiling.
4 Pour over potato mixture; toss lightly until dressing is absorbed. Divide salad among 6 individual bowls or spoon into a large serving bowl; crisscross saved bacon pieces on top. Serve warm.

Summer Garden Potato Salad
Sunny corn, green peas and cherry tomatoes join with potatoes cut into sticks for this colorful salad.
Makes 6 servings

6 medium-size potatoes, pared
1 package (10 ounces) frozen green peas
1 can (12 or 16 ounces) whole-kernel corn, drained
½ cup sliced green onions
1 envelope herb-flavor salad-dressing mix
Cider vinegar
Vegetable oil
1 cup halved cherry tomatoes

There's a potato salad here to please nearly everyone. (From left to right): German Potato Salad Bowls, Sun-Gold Potato Mold, Summer Garden Potato Salad, Swiss Potato Salad Tower. Pick any of them that appeals.

1 head of Boston lettuce
1 tablespoon chopped chives

1 Cut potatoes into ½-inch-thick sticks about 2 inches long. Cook in boiling salted water in a large saucepan 10 minutes, or just until tender; drain, then shake pan gently over low heat to dry potatoes. Place in a large bowl.
2 Cook peas, following label directions; drain. Add to potatoes with corn and onions.
3 Prepare salad-dressing mix with vinegar, water and vegetable oil, following label directions. Drizzle ⅓ cup over potato mixture; toss lightly until dressing is absorbed; cover. Chill several hours to season and blend flavors.
4 Place tomatoes in a small bowl; drizzle 1 tablespoon dressing over; cover. Chill. (Save remaining dressing for salad for another meal.)
5 When ready to serve, line a large salad bowl with lettuce; spoon potato mixture into center and tomatoes around edge. Sprinkle chives over tomatoes.

●

Swiss Potato-Salad Tower
New creamy bouillon-flavor dressing seasons layers of sliced potatoes and red onions.
Makes 6 to 8 servings

2 chicken-bouillon cubes
1 beef-bouillon cube

¼ cup cider vinegar
¼ cup vegetable oil
¼ cup light cream or table cream
12 medium-size potatoes
3 medium-size red onions, sliced and separated into rings
¼ cup chopped parsley
1 teaspoon salt
¼ teaspoon pepper
Leaf lettuce

1 Combine chicken- and beef-bouillon cubes, vinegar, vegetable oil and cream in a jar with tight-fitting lid. Let stand to dissolve bouillon cubes while cooking potatoes.
2 Cook potatoes in boiling salted water in a large saucepan 30 minutes, or just until tender; drain. Peel and slice while still warm; arrange slices in layer in a baking pan lined with wax paper or transparent wrap; top with layer of onion rings.
3 Shake dressing in jar to mix; pour over potatoes and onions; sprinkle with parsley, salt and pepper. Cover with wax paper or transparent wrap; chill several hours or overnight to season and blend flavors.
4 Just before serving, transfer about half of the potatoes and onion rings to a large platter with slotted pancake turner. Repeat with remaining potatoes and onion rings to make a tower shape. Garnish platter with a ruff of leaf lettuce.

1647

FRUIT SALADS

Cantaloupe Coupe
Fluted melon halves hold fruited rice salad.
Makes 6 servings

  3 *small firm ripe cantaloupes*
  3 *cups cooked rice (¾ cup uncooked)*
  ½ *cup sliced celery*
  ½ *cup chopped pecans*
  ½ *cup golden raisins*
  ½ *cup mayonnaise or salad dressing*
  2 *tablespoons honey*
  1 *tablespoon lime juice*
  ¼ *teaspoon ground ginger*
    Bibb or Boston lettuce
  6 *slices boiled ham (from 2 six-ounce pack-ages)*

1 Cut each cantaloupe in half crosswise; scoop out seeds, then make even sawtooth cuts around edge of each. Turn halves upside down on paper toweling to drain; cover; chill.
2 Pare cantaloupe trimmings; dice and combine with rice, celery, pecans and raisins in a large bowl.
3 Blend mayonnaise or salad dressing, honey, lime juice and ginger in a 1-cup measure; pour over rice mixture; toss lightly to mix. Chill at least an hour to season and blend flavors.
4 When ready to serve, run a knife around inside of rind of each melon half to loosen meat, then cut meat into wedges, leaving in place in shell. Place halves on serving plates.
5 Line each with 2 or 3 lettuce leaves; pile rice mixture on top. Cut each ham slice lengthwise into 4 strips; roll each into a rosette; tuck 4 into rice salad in each cantaloupe.

Persimmon Salad
This exotic holidaytime delicacy combines so invitingly with avocado and greens in a lemony dressing.
Makes 8 servings

8 *cups broken mixed salad greens*
1 *firm ripe avocado, halved, peeled, seeded and sliced*
1 *persimmon, stemmed, halved and sliced*
  HONEY DRESSING *(recipe follows)*

1 Place greens in a large salad bowl. Arrange avocado and persimmon slices, alternately, in a ring on top. (Tip: Peel avocado just before serving so it will keep its bright green color.)
2 Drizzle HONEY DRESSING over salad; toss to mix well.
  HONEY DRESSING—Combine ¼ cup olive or

vegetable oil, 2 tablespoons lemon juice, 1 tablespoon honey and ¼ teaspoon salt in a jar with a tight-fitting lid; shake well to mix. Makes about ½ cup.

Double Grapefruit Cup
Sparkly-cool and deliciously tart. Frozen fruit speeds the setting.
Makes 6 servings

1 *package pineapple-grapefruit–flavor gelatin*
¾ *cup hot water*
1 *can (about 14 ounces) frozen grapefruit sections*
¾ *cup cold water*

1 Dissolve gelatin in hot water in a medium-size bowl; add frozen grapefruit, separating pieces of fruit with a fork; stir in cold water.
2 Chill at least 25 minutes, or until softly set.
3 Spoon into glasses or small cups. Garnish with fresh mint, if you wish.

Pagoda Fruits
What a glamorous salad, yet the arrangement is really very simple.
Makes 4 servings

1 *can (8 ounces) pear halves*
1 *can (8 ounces) cling-peach slices*
1 *can (8 ounces) figs*
1 *can (8 ounces) Royal Anne cherries*
1 *jar (5 ounces) blue-cheese spread, well chilled*
  Bibb lettuce
½ *cup mayonnaise or salad dressing*
¼ *cup honey*
2 *teaspoons syrup from fruits*

1 Drain fruits; shape cheese spread into small balls. Chill all.
2 Line a serving plate with lettuce, building up center slightly. Place 4 pear halves around center; fill pear hollows with cheese balls. Thread each of 4 kebab sticks with 2 peach slices, a fig and a cherry; stick into pears. Place remaining fruits around edge.
3 Blend remaining ingredients in a small bowl; serve separately.

Gold Coast Fruit Salad
The popular fruit-and-cheese combination goes to the table salad style.
Makes 8 servings

1 *small fresh pineapple*
2 *cups (1 pint) strawberries*

Avocado Appetizers also double nicely as fruit salads.

Cantaloupe Coupe: fruited rice sprigged with ham rolls.

1 can (1 pound, 13 ounces) pear halves
4 medium-size seedless oranges
1 package (6 ounces) process Gruyere cheese
⅓ cup vegetable oil
3 tablespoons lime juice
2 tablespoons light corn syrup
½ teaspoon grated lime peel
¼ teaspoon salt
1 medium-size head Boston lettuce

1 Pare pineapple; quarter lengthwise; core. Cut fruit into bite-size pieces. Wash strawberries, hull and halve. Drain syrup from pears; slice pears. Pare oranges and section. Cube cheese.
2 Combine vegetable oil, lime juice, corn syrup, lime peel and salt in a jar with a tight-fitting lid; shake well to mix.
3 Line a large salad bowl with lettuce leaves; break remainder into bite-size pieces in center of bowl. Arrange fruits in separate sections around edge on lettuce; pile cheese in center. Pour dressing over all; toss lightly to mix.

Avocado Appetizers
Perfect for a starter course. Nippy mint dressing seasons the fruit-salad filling.
Makes 6 servings

1 can (11 ounces) mandarin-orange segments,
  drained
1 large red apple, quartered, cored and diced
1 large firm ripe banana, peeled and sliced
¼ cup vegetable oil

3 tablespoons lemon juice
1 tablespoon sugar
1 teaspoon chopped fresh mint
¼ teaspoon salt
3 medium-size firm ripe avocados

1 Set aside 12 of the mandarin-orange segments for garnish. Combine remaining with diced apple and banana in a medium-size bowl.
2 Combine vegetable oil, lemon juice, sugar, mint and salt in a small jar with a tight-fitting lid; shake well to mix. Pour 2 tablespoons over fruits; toss lightly to mix.
3 Halve avocados lengthwise, and pit but do not peel; trim a thin slice from rounded side of each, if needed, to make it set flat; place on serving plates.
4 Brush hollow of each with part of the remaining dressing; fill with fruit mixture. Thread saved mandarin-orange segments onto wooden picks and stick, kebab style, into salads; garnish with mint sprigs, if you wish. Serve with remaining dressing.

1649

Spring Salad Bowl
Tangy pineapple and mellow avocado with greens make this refreshing salad.
Makes 8 servings

1 can (about 14 ounces) frozen pineapple
  chunks, thawed
1 large firm ripe avocado
8 cups broken salad greens

¼ cup vegetable oil
2 tablespoons cider vinegar
½ teaspoon salt
½ teaspoon paprika
¼ teaspoon ground ginger

1 Drain syrup from pineapple into a cup and set aside for Step 3. Halve avocado; remove pit and peel, then cut into thin slices.
2 Place greens in a large salad bowl; arrange avocado slices in a ring on top; mound pineapple chunks in center.
3 Combine 2 tablespoonfuls of the saved pineapple syrup with remaining ingredients in a jar with a tight-fitting lid; shake well to mix. Drizzle over salad; toss lightly to mix.

Frosted Pineapple Royale
This golden fruit makes such a pretty server, and here it's heaped with cubes of frozen fruit salad.
Makes 6 servings

1 package (8 ounces) cream cheese, softened
½ cup mayonnaise or salad dressing
2 tablespoons 10X (confectioners' powdered) sugar
1 tablespoon lime juice
1 cup tiny marshmallows
1 cup orange sections
1 cup fresh peach slices
½ cup halved green grapes
½ cup chopped toasted slivered almonds (from a 5-ounce can)
¼ cup sliced maraschino cherries
1 cup cream for whipping
3 small ripe pineapples

1 Beat cream cheese with mayonnaise or salad dressing, 10X sugar and lime juice until smooth in a large bowl; stir in marshmallows, orange sections, peach slices, grapes, almonds and cherries.
2 Beat cream until stiff in a medium-size bowl; fold into cheese-fruit mixture. Pour into a shallow dish, 8x8x2; cover. Freeze several hours, or until firm.
3 Halve each pineapple lengthwise, cutting through leafy crown; cut out core, then cut fruit from rind of each half in one piece; lift out.
4 Slice enough of the fruit crosswise to make 42 thin strips; stand 7, overlapping, in each shell; chill. (Save any remaining fruit to dice and add to fruit cup for another meal.)
5 Remove fruit salad from freezer 15 minutes before serving and let stand at room temperature to soften, then cut into 1-inch cubes. Pile into pineapple shells.

1650

Frozen Fruit Salad
Cooling and refreshing—serve as dessert or salad.
Makes 6 servings

2 ripe bananas
1 can (6 ounces) pineapple juice
2 tablespoons lemon juice
1 cup orange juice
½ cup mayonnaise or salad dressing
1 can (10 ounces) mandarin oranges
¼ cup sugar
Iceberg lettuce

1 Combine bananas, pineapple juice and lemon juice in electric-blender container; whirl 1 minute at low speed until smooth.
2 Add orange juice, mayonnaise or salad dressing, mandarin oranges (undrained) and sugar; whirl ½ minute at low speed.
3 Pour into 6 six-ounce molds, or into a 9x9x2-inch pan. Freeze about 4 hours, or until firm.
4 To unmold: Loosen at top edge with a sharp knife, then dip *very quickly* in and out of a pan of hot water; cover mold with serving plate; turn upside down; gently lift off mold. If molded in pan, cut into squares. Serve with lettuce and with additional mayonnaise or salad dressing, if you wish.

MOLDED SALADS

TO MAKE A PERFECT JELLIED MOLD:

Mixing—Follow directions carefully when dissolving gelatin, as mixture should be sparkling-smooth, with no tiny granules clinging to bowl.

Fruit-flavor gelatin dissolves quickly in hot water. Unflavored gelatin can be dissolved either of these two ways: (1) Soften in cold water, then dissolve in a hot liquid or heat softened gelatin over hot water (as in a double boiler) until dissolved; or (2) mix dry gelatin with sugar, then add liquid and heat, following recipe directions.

Chilling—Place dissolved gelatin in the refrigerator to chill until syrupy-thick (consistency should be like an unbeaten egg white). Gelatin sets first at the bottom and sides of bowl, so stir occasionally for even thickening.

In a hurry? Follow suggestions on package label or hasten setting either of these ways: (1) Pour gelatin mixture into a shallow pan and place in refrigerator, or (2) set bowl of gelatin mixture in a larger bowl of ice and water. Keep

Jeweled gelatins: Curried-Chicken Coronet and Rainbow Fruit Mold (front), Tomato-Aspic Crown (behind).

on the kitchen counter where you can watch it, as it jells fast.

Gelatin get away from you and set too quickly? Place bowl over simmering water and heat, stirring constantly, until melted. Then start chilling again, as if freshly mixed.

Layering—Like a fancy design on top? Place mold in a larger pan of ice and water (pan should be deep enough so ice and water will come to within one inch of top of mold). Spoon about a ¼-inch-thick layer of syrupy gelatin into a mold and chill just until beginning to be sticky-firm. Arrange foods to make the design you wish on top of it; carefully spoon in another thin gelatin layer barely to cover; chill just until *sticky-firm*. This is important whenever you add one layer on top of another, so layers will hold together. This way a layered mold will turn out beautifully firm without one layer's slipping from another.

Make any remaining layers this way: Keep rest of gelatin syrupy-thick. (On a cool day keep it at room temperature, or watch it if it is necessary to keep it refrigerated.) Fold in other recipe ingredients, then spoon mixture carefully on top of the already-set layer while it is still sticky-firm.

Setting—Place mold in a far corner of your refrigerator where it can chill without being disturbed. Most molds can be turned out at their prettiest if chilled overnight. Large ones, or those heavy with fruits or vegetables, need at least 12 hours' chilling. Usually small molds are firm enough to turn out after 3 to 4 hours' chilling.

HOW TO UNMOLD A JELLIED SALAD

1 Be sure salad is firm. Run a knife around top to loosen, then dip mold *very quickly* in and out of hot water. This quick heating is just enough to free the bottom.

2 Set your serving plate upside down on top of mold. Then, holding plate and mold firmly with both hands, flip right side up with a mere twist of the wrists.

1652

3 Lift off mold and your prize is ready to garnish. Another tip: If you moisten plate with water first, you can slide salad easily if it's off center on the plate.

Curried-Chicken Coronet
A partylike rich chicken-salad mousse delicately spiced with curry.
Makes 8 servings

2 *whole chicken breasts (about 2 pounds)*
2 *cups water*
1 *medium-size onion, sliced*
  Handful of celery tops
1 *teaspoon salt (for chicken)*
3 *peppercorns*
1 *envelope unflavored gelatin*
2 *eggs, separated*
½ *cup chopped toasted almonds*
1 *teaspoon curry powder*
½ *teaspoon salt (for salad)*
¼ *teaspoon pepper*
1 *cup mayonnaise*
1 *cup cream for whipping*
1 *can (about 13 ounces) frozen pineapple chunks, thawed and drained*
½ *cup flaked coconut*

1 Combine chicken breasts, water, onion, celery tops, 1 teaspoon salt and peppercorns in large saucepan; simmer, covered, 45 minutes, or until chicken is tender. Let stand until cool enough to handle, then skin chicken and take meat from bones. Dice chicken fine (you should have about 2 cups).
2 Strain stock into a bowl; measure out 1 cupful; pour into a medium-size saucepan and cool. (Use any remaining stock for soup for another day.)
3 Soften gelatin in cooled stock in saucepan; heat, stirring constantly, just until dissolved.
4 Beat egg yolks slightly in small bowl; slowly stir in dissolved gelatin. Return mixture to saucepan and cook, stirring constantly, 1 minute, or until slightly thickened; remove from heat.
5 Stir in diced chicken, almonds, curry powder, ½ teaspoon salt and pepper, blending well. Chill 30 minutes, or until mixture is syrupy-thick; blend in mayonnaise.
6 Beat egg whites until stiff in large bowl; fold in chicken mixture until no streaks of white remain.
7 Beat cream until stiff in medium-size bowl; fold into chicken mixture.
8 Pour into a 6-cup ring mold; chill several hours, or until firm.
9 Unmold onto serving plate; fit a shallow bowl into center of mold; fill with drained pineapple chunks; sprinkle with coconut.

Tomato-Aspic Crown
Tartly seasoned relish in a no-fuss aspic ring to go with the chicken-salad mold.
Makes 8 servings

3 envelopes unflavored gelatin
3 cups water
3 cans (8 ounces each) tomato sauce
1 tablespoon lemon juice
  FRESH VEGETABLE RELISH (recipe follows)

1 Soften gelatin in 1 cup water in medium-size saucepan; heat slowly, stirring constantly, just until dissolved. Stir in remaining 2 cups water, tomato sauce and lemon juice.
2 Pour into a 6-cup ring mold; chill several hours, or until firm.
3 Unmold onto serving plate; fill center with FRESH VEGETABLE RELISH.
  FRESH VEGETABLE RELISH—Wash and stem 2 cups (1 pint) cherry tomatoes. Combine with 1 cup sliced crisp celery, 1 cup diced green pepper and 1 cup coarsely chopped Bermuda onion in a large bowl. Drizzle with ⅓ cup lemon juice; toss lightly. Chill at least 1 hour. Makes about 4 cups.

Cucumber-Cream Mold
Makes 6 servings

1 package (3 ounces) lemon-flavor gelatin
¾ cup hot water
½ cup cold water
2 tablespoons lemon juice
1 teaspoon salt
⅛ teaspoon pepper
1 medium-size cucumber
2 medium-size carrots, pared
  1 ripe olive
1 tablespoon chopped parsley
1 teaspoon grated onion
1 cup dairy sour cream
  Watercress

1 Dissolve gelatin in hot water in medium-size bowl; stir in cold water, lemon juice, salt and pepper. Spoon a thin layer into 4-cup mold or dish; set mold in larger pan of ice and water to speed setting. Chill until just beginning to be sticky-firm. (Keep remaining gelatin at room temperature.)
2 Slice half the cucumber very thin; arrange slices, overlapping, in ring on sticky-firm gelatin in mold. Cut 5 thin slices from a carrot and 1 slice from ripe olive; arrange in center of cucumber ring to make a flower design. Carefully spoon in another thin layer of gelatin; let set until sticky-firm.
3 Pare and chop remaining cucumber and grate carrots into small bowl. Stir in parsley and onion, then sour cream; fold into remaining gelatin. Spoon over chilled gelatin in mold; remove from ice; chill until firm.
4 Unmold by first loosening around edge with thin-blade knife, then dipping quickly in and out of a pan of hot water. Invert onto serving plate; garnish with watercress.

Boston Beanie Ring
Summertime's picnic favorite puts on molded salad airs. Serve with frankfurters or grilled hamburgers.
Makes 6 servings

1 cup tomato juice
1 package (3 ounces) lemon-flavor gelatin
⅓ cup catsup
3 tablespoons lemon juice
1 teaspoon prepared mustard
½ teaspoon salt
1 can (1 pound) baked beans in tomato sauce
½ cup diced celery
¼ cup drained sweet-pickle relish
  Small inner romaine leaves

1 Heat tomato juice to boiling in a small saucepan; pour over gelatin in a medium-size bowl; stir until gelatin dissolves.
2 Stir in catsup, lemon juice, mustard and salt. Chill 30 minutes, or until as thick as unbeaten egg white.
3 Fold in baked beans, celery and pickle relish; spoon into a 5-cup ring mold. Chill several hours, or until firm. (Overnight is best.)
4 When ready to serve, run a sharp-tip thin-blade knife around top of salad, then dip mold very quickly in and out of a pan of hot water. Cover mold with a serving plate; turn upside down; carefully lift off mold. Stand romaine leaves in center of ring.

Aspic-Bean Molds
Green beans give individual jellied tomato salads a different flavor lift.
Makes 6 servings

Boston Beanie Ring, new variation of an old favorite.

Jeweled Honeydew Mold mixes melon and strawberries.

1654

1 envelope unflavored gelatin
2 cups tomato juice
2 tablespoons lemon juice
Few drops liquid red pepper seasoning
½ teaspoon salt
1 cup crisply cooked cut green beans
Iceberg lettuce
1½ teaspoons mayonnaise

1 Soften gelatin in ½ cup of the tomato juice in a medium-size saucepan; heat slowly, stirring constantly, until gelatin dissolves; remove from heat. Stir in remaining tomato juice, lemon juice, liquid red pepper seasoning and salt. Chill until as thick as unbeaten egg white.

2 Fold in green beans; spoon into 6 individual molds or 5-ounce custard cups. Chill several hours, or until firm. When ready to serve, unmold onto lettuce-lined plates. Top each with mayonnaise.

Coleslaw-Relish Mold
Makes 6 servings

2 packages (3 ounces each) lemon-flavor gelatin
2 cups boiling water
1½ cups cold water
½ cup finely shredded green pepper
1 cup finely shredded pared carrot
⅔ cup mayonnaise or salad dressing
2 tablespoons sugar
¼ teaspoon salt
3 tablespoons milk
4 teaspoons cider vinegar
3 cups coarsely shredded cabbage
Chicory or curly endive

1 Dissolve gelatin in boiling water in a medium-size bowl; stir in cold water. Measure ½ cup into a 6-cup mold and set aside for next step. Measure 1 cup into a small bowl. Chill gelatin mixture in medium-size bowl 30 minutes, and gelatin mixture in small bowl 20 minutes, or until as thick as unbeaten egg white.
2 Place mold in a pan of ice and water to speed setting. Chill layer until as thick as unbeaten egg white; stir in green pepper. Continue chilling *just* until sticky-firm.
3 Stir carrot into thickened gelatin in small bowl; spoon over pepper layer in mold. Chill *just* until sticky-firm.
4 While carrot layer chills, beat mayonnaise or salad dressing, sugar, salt, milk and vinegar into thickened gelatin in medium-size bowl; fold in cabbage; spoon over carrot layer in mold. Remove from ice and water. Chill in refrigerator 6 hours, or until firm.
5 Unmold onto a serving plate; frame with chicory or endive leaves. Garnish mold with several green-pepper "petals" and a carrot curl threaded onto a wooden pick.

Lemon Beet Mold
Makes 6 servings

1 package (3 ounces) lemon-flavor gelatin
1 cup boiling water
1 cup cold water
2 tablespoons lemon juice
1 can (1 pound) diced beets, drained
¼ cup chopped green onions
PARSLEY DRESSING (recipe follows)

1 Dissolve gelatin in boiling water in a medium-size bowl; stir in cold water and lemon juice. Chill 50 minutes, or just until as thick as unbeaten egg white.
2 Fold in beets and onions; spoon into a 4-cup mold. Chill several hours, or until firm.
3 Unmold onto a serving plate; garnish with romaine, if you wish, and serve with PARSLEY DRESSING.

PARSLEY DRESSING—Blend ½ cup mayonnaise or salad dressing with 2 tablespoons cream and 2 tablespoons chopped parsley in a small bowl.

●

Appetizer Madrilène Cups
Layers of paper-thin vegetable slices seem to float in this shimmering soup-appetizer.
Makes 6 servings

1 envelope unflavored gelatin
1½ cups water
1 chicken-bouillon cube
1 can (12 ounces) jellied madrilène
6 small radishes, thinly sliced
1 small cucumber, thinly sliced
1 medium-size carrot, pared and thinly sliced
6 thin slices of lime

1 Soften gelatin in 1 cup water in small saucepan; add bouillon cube. Heat, stirring constantly, until gelatin and cube are dissolved.
2 Remove from heat; stir in remaining ½ cup water and madrilène; chill 1 hour, or until syrupy-thick.
3 Place 6 six-ounce custard cups or molds in a shallow pan of ice and water. Spoon 1 tablespoon syrupy gelatin into each cup; let set until just beginning to be sticky-firm, then arrange a layer of sliced radishes, overlapping, in gelatin. Carefully spoon in 2 tablespoons more syrupy gelatin, and again let set until sticky-firm.
4 Repeat, making a layer of cucumber slices and 2 tablespoons syrupy gelatin, then one of carrot slices and 3 tablespoons syrupy gelatin for each. Remove from pan of ice and water and chill until firm.
5 Unmold onto serving dishes; garnish each with a twist of sliced lime. Serve plain, or with a cut stalk of Belgian endive and crisp crackers, if you wish.

●

Raspberry Chiffon Royale
Serve this double-tier pink party special with your favorite cookies.
Makes 8 to 12 servings

1 envelope unflavored gelatin
¾ cup sugar
½ cup water

4 eggs, separated
1 can (6 ounces) frozen concentrate for raspberry-lemon punch or pink lemonade
1 cup cream for whipping
Red food coloring
Fresh red raspberries

1 Mix gelatin with ½ cup sugar in top of small double boiler (save remaining ¼ cup sugar for Step 4); stir in water.
2 Beat egg yolks slightly in small bowl; stir into gelatin mixture. Cook over simmering water, stirring constantly, 5 minutes, or until gelatin is dissolved and mixture coats a metal spoon.
3 Remove from heat; pour into large bowl; stir in frozen concentrate until completely melted.
4 Beat egg whites until foamy in medium-size bowl; gradually beat in remaining ¼ cup sugar, a tablespoon at a time, until meringue forms soft peaks. Fold into gelatin mixture.
5 Beat cream until stiff in same bowl, then fold into gelatin-meringue mixture until no streaks of white remain.
6 Tint mixture pale pink with a few drops of red food coloring, then measure out 2 cups and tint a deeper pink with a drop or two more.
7 Spoon deeper-pink mixture into an 8-cup mold; chill 15 minutes, or just until sticky-firm. Spoon remaining lighter-pink mixture on top; chill several hours, or until firm.
8 Unmold onto serving plate; garnish top with crown of fresh raspberries.

Rainbow Fruit Mold
Three color-bright layers, each with a tangy fruit, make this a handsome salad-dessert.
Makes 8 to 12 servings

1 package (3 ounces) lemon-flavor gelatin
1 package (3 ounces) strawberry-flavor gelatin
1 package (3 ounces) orange-flavor gelatin
3 cups hot water
2¼ cups cold water
½ cup drained canned sliced peaches (from an 8-ounce can)
1 cup sliced ripe firm strawberries
1 can (about 11 ounces) mandarin-orange sections, drained
1 cup cream for whipping

1 Mix and chill each fruit-flavor gelatin, one at a time and 15 minutes apart, this way: Start with lemon-flavor gelatin, then strawberry and then orange; dissolve each in 1 cup hot water in a

1655

shallow pan, then stir ¾ cup cold water into each; chill until syrupy-thick. (The time intervals of 15 minutes are important so all gelatins do not become syrupy at once.)

2 As soon as lemon gelatin is syrupy-thick, place an 8-cup bowl (we used a kitchen mixing bowl) in a larger bowl of ice and water; pour ½ cup syrupy gelatin into bowl and make a design of peach slices on top.

3 Let layer set a few minutes, or until sticky-firm, then gradually spoon ¾ cup more syrupy lemon gelatin over peaches. (Pour remaining ½ cup lemon gelatin into orange-flavor gelatin that is chilling. This will make all layers look of equal depth when mold is turned out.) Let lemon-peach layer set until sticky-firm, keeping bowl in bowl of ice until all layers have been added.

4 Next, fold sliced strawberries into syrupy strawberry gelatin; carefully spoon on top of sticky-firm lemon-peach layer in bowl, pushing some berries to edge so fruit will show when unmolded; let stand until sticky-firm.

5 Fold mandarin-orange sections into orange-gelatin mixture; carefully spoon into mold, pushing some sections to edge; don't move until set, as bowl is filled to the top (add ice if needed). Remove bowl from ice water; chill overnight, or until very firm.

6 Beat cream until stiff in medium-size bowl. Unmold gelatin onto serving plate; top with some whipped cream; serve remaining to spoon over.

Jeweled Honeydew Mold

Thin melon crescents and strawberries shine through rosy gelatin for this salad-dessert to serve with a creamy lemon topper.
Makes 8 servings

1656

1 package (6 ounces) strawberry-flavor gelatin
1 package (3 ounces) lemon-flavor gelatin
3 cups hot water
2 cups cold water
½ medium-size honeydew melon
½ cup sliced hulled strawberries
½ cup cream for whipping
½ teaspoon vanilla
½ cup lemon sherbet, softened slightly

1 Dissolve strawberry and lemon gelatins in hot water in a large bowl; stir in cold water. Pour ½ cup into a lightly oiled 6-cup bowl. Place bowl in a pan of ice and water to speed setting; chill until softly set. Keep remaining gelatin mixture at room temperature for Step 3.

2 Scoop seeds from honeydew melon; slice half

into 8 thin wedges; pare each, then trim off inside of each slice, leaving a band about ¼ inch thick. Dice trimmings and set aside with remaining melon for Steps 4 and 5.

3 Place the 8 melon slices, spoke fashion, in softly set gelatin in bowl so slices meet in center; carefully spoon in another ½ cup gelatin mixture; chill until sticky-firm. Trim top edge of slices even with bowl so salad will stand flat when turned out.

4 While mold chills, chill remaining gelatin mixture in refrigerator 30 minutes, or until as thick as unbeaten egg white; fold in diced honeydew from Step 2 and strawberries; carefully spoon into mold. Remove from pan of ice and water. Chill in refrigerator several hours, or until firm. (Overnight is even better.)

5 Cut balls from remaining melon with a melon-ball cutter or ¼ teaspoon of a measuring-spoon set.

6 When ready to serve, run a sharp-tip thin-blade knife carefully around top of bowl, then dip bowl *quickly* in and out of a pan of hot water. Cover with a serving plate; turn upside down; carefully lift off bowl. Garnish with melon balls.

7 Beat cream with vanilla until stiff in a small bowl; fold in softened sherbet. Serve separately to spoon over salad.

Lemon Berry Mold

Serve this salad-dessert with a tangy-sweet topper.
Makes 6 servings

2 envelopes unflavored gelatin
1 cup sugar
½ teaspoon salt
3½ cups water
½ cup lemon juice
  Yellow food coloring
1 pint strawberries, washed and stemmed
  CHEESE FLUFF *(recipe follows)*

1 Soften gelatin with sugar and salt in 1 cup of the water in a small saucepan; heat, stirring constantly, just until gelatin dissolves.

2 Pour into a medium-size bowl; stir in remaining 2½ cups water and lemon juice; tint lemon-yellow with food coloring.

3 Make a design on top of mold this way: Pour a one-inch depth of gelatin mixture into a 6-cup mold; chill along with remaining gelatin in bowl until layer is as thick as unbeaten egg white. Arrange a ring of strawberries, pointed ends out, in gelatin in mold; chill until sticky-firm.

4 Fold remaining strawberries, saving one for garnish, into thickened gelatin in bowl; spoon over sticky-firm layer in mold. Chill several hours, or until firm.

5 Unmold onto serving plate; top with saved strawberry. Serve with CHEESE FLUFF.

CHEESE FLUFF—Soften 1 package (3 or 4 ounces) cream cheese in a small bowl. Beat ½ cup cream for whipping with 1 tablespoon sugar until stiff in a second small bowl; fold into cheese. Makes about 1¼ cups.

Sweet enough for dessert: frozen Party Fruit Tower.

Party Fruit Tower

Star this frozen beauty as salad and dessert, as it's rich.
Makes 8 to 10 servings

    1 can (1 pound) apricot halves
    1 can (1 pound) cling-peach slices
    1 package (3 ounces) strawberry-flavor gela-
        tin
    1 cup hot water
    2 tablespoons lemon juice
    1 package (8 ounces) cream cheese
    ½ cup mayonnaise or salad dressing
    ½ cup cream for whipping
    1½ cups tiny marshmallows
    ½ cup sliced maraschino cherries

1 Drain syrups from apricots and peaches into a 2-cup measure. Cut fruits into small pieces and set aside for Step 5.
2 Dissolve gelatin in hot water in a 4-cup measure; stir in 1¼ cups of the fruit syrup and lemon juice; cool to lukewarm.
3 Beat cream cheese until soft and smooth in a large bowl; blend in mayonnaise or salad dressing, then gelatin mixture. Set bowl in a pan of ice and water to speed setting. Chill at room temperature, stirring often, just until as thick as unbeaten egg white.
4 While gelatin mixture chills, beat cream until stiff in a small bowl.
5 Fold cut apricots and peaches, marshmallows and cherries into thickened gelatin mixture, then gently fold in whipped cream until mixture starts to mound softly. Spoon into an 8-cup mold. Freeze six hours, or until firm. (Overnight is best.)
6 When ready to serve, run a sharp-tip thin-blade knife around top of salad, then dip mold *very quickly* in and out of a pan of hot water. Cover mold with a serving plate; turn upside down; carefully lift off mold. Garnish salad and plate with watercress or small crisp lettuce leaves, if you wish.

Raspberry Chiffon Royale.

1657

MAIN DISH SALADS

Summer Potato "Chowder"

Creamy bouillon dressing seasons vegetables while still warm for this salad twist on an old-timer.
Makes 6 servings

    6 large potatoes
    1 cup chopped green onions
    2 cans (1 pound each) sliced carrots
    2 envelopes instant chicken broth

1 teaspoon salt
1 teaspoon leaf basil, crumbled
¼ cup vegetable oil
¼ cup cider vinegar
¼ cup light cream or table cream
6 cups broken chicory or curly endive
2 packages (6 ounces each) sliced spiced ham
6 slices process American cheese (from an 8-ounce package)

1 Cook potatoes in boiling salted water in a large saucepan 30 minutes, or just until tender; drain; cool until easy to handle, then peel and slice thin. Layer with about three quarters of the green onions into a shallow dish.

2 Heat carrots to boiling in a medium-size saucepan; drain. Layer with remaining onions into a second shallow dish.

3 Combine chicken broth, salt, basil, vegetable oil, vinegar and cream in a jar with a tight-fitting lid; shake well to mix. Pour about ¾ over potato mixture and remaining over carrots. Chill at least 2 hours to season and blend flavors.

4 Divide chicory among 6 soup plates or shallow salad bowls; layer potato and carrot mixtures on top.

5 Stack each two slices of spiced ham with a slice of cheese between; cut in quarters, then cut each quarter in half diagonally to make triangles; arrange on top of salads. Garnish with parsley, if you wish.

Shrimps-Louis Dinner Salad
The summeriest of salads, with chunks of shrimps in a creamy dressing.
Makes 6 servings

½ pound raw shrimps
OR: 1 can (about 5 ounces) deveined cooked shrimps
¼ cup mayonnaise
¼ cup dairy sour cream
2 tablespoons chili sauce
1 teaspoon lime juice
½ teaspoon sugar
½ teaspoon grated onion
¼ teaspoon seasoned salt
1 large head of iceberg lettuce, broken into bite-size pieces (about 9 cups)

1 Shell and remove sand vein from fresh shrimps; simmer gently in water just to cover in small saucepan 3 to 5 minutes, or just until shrimps are pink. Drain; cool, then dice. (If using canned shrimps, rinse under running cold water before cutting up.)

1658

2 Combine shrimps with remaining ingredients, except lettuce, in medium-size bowl; cover; chill at least 30 minutes before serving.

3 Fill a large salad bowl with lettuce; pour shrimp dressing over; toss to coat greens well.

⬤

Supper Salad
Makes 6 servings

2 packages (10 ounces each) frozen lima beans
1 medium-size onion, chopped (½ cup)
2 stalks celery, sliced
6 slices bacon, cut in pieces
¼ cup bacon drippings
¼ cup wine vinegar or cider vinegar
¼ teaspoon pepper
½ pound salami, cut into thin strips
1 package (8 ounces) sliced Swiss or American cheese, cut into thin strips
½ cup halved pitted ripe olives
3 medium-size carrots, pared and coarsely grated
3 slices sweet onion, separated into rings
Few leaves of romaine
½ teaspoon salt
Dash of paprika
Vegetable oil and cider vinegar

1 Cook frozen lima beans, following label directions; drain. Place in salad bowl; add onion and celery.

2 Sauté bacon until crisp in medium-size frying pan; drain on paper toweling. Measure ¼ cup drippings; mix with ¼ cup vinegar and pepper; pour over lima beans in bowl; add bacon; toss lightly.

3 Arrange salami, cheese, olives and carrots in separate piles on top; place onion rings in middle; edge salad bowl with romaine.

4 Sprinkle salt and paprika over. Toss lightly, adding a little oil and vinegar, if needed.

Bouillabaisse Salad
Three seafood treats—scallops, salmon and haddock—go with vegetables and greens in a tomato-rich dressing.
Makes 6 servings

1 pound fresh sea scallops
OR: 2 packages (7 ounces each) frozen sea scallops
1 slice onion
1 slice lemon

Meaty main dish salads (l. to r.): Bouillabaisse Salad, Garden Vegetable Bounty and Summer Potato Chowder.

1   teaspoon salt
1   package (1 pound) frozen haddock fillets
    PIQUANT TOMATO DRESSING (recipe follows)
2   packages (9 ounces each) frozen artichoke
    hearts
2   packages (9 ounces each) frozen Italian
    green beans
6   cups broken salad greens
1   can (about 8 ounces) salmon, drained, boned
    and cut in chunks
6   small ripe tomatoes, peeled and cut in
    wedges
1   lemon, cut in 6 wedges

1 Wash fresh scallops in cold water; drain. (No need to thaw frozen ones.)
2 Fill a large frying pan with a 1-inch depth of water; season with onion, lemon and salt; heat to boiling. Add scallops; cover; remove from heat. Let stand 5 minutes for fresh scallops and 10 minutes for frozen ones; lift out with a slotted spoon and place in a large shallow dish.
3 Heat same pan of water to boiling again; add frozen haddock; cover. Simmer 5 minutes; remove from heat; let stand 5 minutes. Lift out with a wide spatula and place in dish with scallops. Drizzle each with ¼ cup of the PIQUANT TOMATO DRESSING; cover; chill.
4 Cook frozen artichoke hearts and Italian green beans in separate saucepans, following label directions; drain. Place in mounds in a

large shallow dish. Drizzle each with ¼ cup of the PIQUANT TOMATO DRESSING; cover; chill.
5 When ready to serve, place 1 cup of the greens in each of 6 soup plates or shallow salad bowls. Cut haddock into ½-inch cubes; place with scallops, artichoke hearts, and green beans in separate mounds in each plate; pile salmon in centers. Tuck tomato wedges between fish and vegetables. Sprinkle scallops with chopped parsley, and haddock with paprika, if you wish. Serve with lemon wedges and remaining PIQUANT TOMATO DRESSING.

PIQUANT TOMATO DRESSING—Combine 1 cup olive oil or vegetable oil; ½ cup wine vinegar or cider vinegar; ½ cup tomato juice; 1 clove garlic, crushed; 2 teaspoons salt; 2 teaspoons sugar; and 1 teaspoon crushed fennel seeds in a jar with a tight-fitting lid; shake well to mix. Makes 2 cups.

1659

Garden Vegetable Bounty
How invitingly colorful it looks with rings of seasoned vegetables, spinach, shredded red cabbage and bologna strips.
Makes 6 servings

1   bag (1½ pounds) frozen mixed vegetables
⅔   cup bottled thin French dressing
1   package (10 ounces) fresh spinach
1   small head red cabbage (about 1½ pounds)

1 cup chopped celery
½ pound piece bologna, cut in thin strips
⅓ cup mayonnaise or salad dressing
4 teaspoons prepared mustard

1 Cook frozen vegetables in boiling salted water, following label directions; drain. Combine with ⅓ cup of the French dressing in a medium-size bowl; toss lightly to mix. Chill at least an hour to season and blend flavors. (Set remaining dressing aside for Step 5.)
2 Remove stems and any coarse ribs from spinach; wash leaves; dry well. Shred red cabbage fine.
3 Arrange spinach around edges in 6 soup plates or shallow salad bowls; place red cabbage in a ring around the spinach.
4 Stir celery into mixed vegetables; spoon into centers. Arrange bologna strips around vegetables.
5 Beat remaining ⅓ cup French dressing into mayonnaise or salad dressing and mustard in a small bowl. Serve separately with salads.

Cornucopia Salad Bowl is almost too beautiful to eat.

Rijsttafel Salad Platter

What a show-off! Everyone takes his choice of eight toppings to eat with tuna and salad-seasoned rice.
Makes 6 servings

1½ cups uncooked regular rice
½ teaspoon curry powder
¼ cup bottled thin French dressing
½ cup mayonnaise or salad dressing
2 cans (7 ounces each) tuna, drained
1 can (about 9 ounces) pineapple tidbits, drained
½ cup sliced green onions
½ cup roasted diced almonds (from a 5-ounce can)
1 cup sliced celery
3 hard-cooked eggs, shelled and chopped
½ cup chopped radishes
½ cup toasted flaked coconut (from an about-4-ounce package)
1 small avocado, peeled, halved, pitted and diced

1 Cook rice, following label directions; drain; place in a medium-size bowl. Stir curry powder into French dressing in a cup; drizzle over hot rice; toss lightly to mix. Chill at least an hour to season.
2 When ready to serve, stir in mayonnaise or salad dressing; spoon onto a large platter.
3 Separate tuna into chunks; mound on top of rice salad in center of platter; pile pineapple tidbits, onions, almonds, celery, eggs, radishes, coconut and avocado, spoke fashion, around edge. Garnish tuna with a radish rose, if you wish. Serve with more French dressing.

Cornucopia Salad Bowl
Makes 6 servings

2 cans (16 ounces each) hominy, drained
1 can (12 or 16 ounces) whole-kernel corn, drained
1 cup diced celery
½ cup sliced green onions
6 tablespoons bottled thin French dressing
½ teaspoon salt
¼ teaspoon pepper
1 package frozen Italian green beans
1 head of Boston lettuce
½ cup prepared sandwich spread
1 package (8 ounces) sliced salami

1 Combine hominy, corn, celery, green onions, 4 tablespoons of the French dressing, salt and pepper in a large bowl; chill at least an hour to season and blend flavors.

2 Cook green beans, following label directions; drain. Combine in a small bowl with remaining 2 tablespoons French dressing; chill along with hominy mixture.

3 When ready to serve, line a large shallow bowl with lettuce; shred any remaining and place in bottom of bowl. Stir sandwich spread into hominy mixture; mound on top of shredded lettuce.

4 Fold salami slices into cornucopia shapes, or cut into strips or small pieces; arrange in a circle on top. Pile seasoned green beans in center. Garnish with a twist of pimiento, if you wish.

Chicken Salad Deluxe

Tender chicken is brightly flavored with a sour-cream–mayonnaise combination.
Makes 4 servings

1 broiler-fryer (about 3 pounds)
4 cups water
1 small onion, sliced
    Few celery tops
¼ teaspoon salt
⅓ cup mayonnaise or salad dressing
⅓ cup dairy sour cream
1 tablespoon lemon juice
¼ teaspoon pepper
¾ cup chopped celery
1 medium-size onion, chopped (½ cup)
¼ cup chopped dill pickle
    Lettuce
    Paprika

1 Combine chicken with water, sliced onion, celery tops and salt in a kettle or Dutch oven. Heat to boiling; reduce heat; cover; simmer about 1 hour, or until chicken is tender. Remove from broth and cool until easy to handle. (Save broth to start a soup another day.)

2 Skin the chicken and take meat from bones. Cut meat into bite-size pieces; put in medium-size bowl.

3 Blend mayonnaise or salad dressing, sour cream, lemon juice and pepper in a small bowl. Combine celery, onion and dill pickle with chicken; add the dressing; toss until evenly coated. Cover; chill at least an hour to season and blend flavors.

4 Line salad bowl with lettuce leaves. Spoon salad into bowl. Sprinkle with paprika.

Salad Niçoise

A refreshingly simple salad that may be prepared earlier in the day, then assembled and served.
Makes 6 servings

5 medium-size potatoes, cooked, drained and cooled
½ pound fresh green beans, cooked, drained and cooled
⅔ cup vegetable oil or olive oil
⅓ cup wine vinegar
2 cloves garlic, crushed
1 tablespoon prepared mustard
1 tablespoon chopped parsley
½ teaspoon instant minced onion
1 teaspoon salt
¼ teaspoon ground pepper
2 large tomatoes, cut into slices
1 red onion, cubed
1 small green pepper, seeded and cubed
6 ripe olives, halved
3 hard-cooked eggs, shelled and sliced
1 can (2 ounces) anchovy fillets, drained
2 medium-size heads of romaine
1 can (14 ounces) tuna fish, drained

1 Peel potatoes and cut into thick slices. Place in a shallow dish. Place beans in a second shallow dish.

2 Combine oil, vinegar, garlic, mustard, parsley, onion, salt and pepper in a jar with a tight-fitting lid; shake well to mix. Drizzle ½ cup over potatoes and 2 tablespoonfuls over beans; let each stand at least 30 minutes to season.

3 Layer vegetables, eggs, anchovies and romaine in a large salad bowl. Break tuna into chunks; arrange on top. Pour rest of dressing over; toss lightly.

SALAD DRESSINGS

Classic French Dressing
Makes 1 cup

Combine ⅔ cup vegetable or olive oil, ½ cup cider or wine vinegar, ½ teaspoon sugar, 1 teaspoon salt and ¼ teaspoon pepper in a screwtop jar with a tight-fitting lid. Shake well to blend; chill. Great for green salads.

Herbed French Dressing
Makes 1 cup

Combine 1 cup CLASSIC FRENCH DRESSING with ½ teaspoon leaf basil, crumbled, ½ teaspoon leaf tarragon, crumbled and 2 tablespoons grated Parmesan cheese in a screw-top jar with tight-fitting lid. Shake well to blend; chill. Refreshing for crispy vegetable salads.

1661

Classic dressing for a classic salad: oil and vinegar.

Tangy French Dressing
Makes 1 cup

Combine 1 cup CLASSIC FRENCH DRESSING with 1 teaspoon Worcestershire sauce; 1 teaspoon prepared mustard; 1 clove of garlic, peeled and halved, in a screw-top jar with a tight-fitting lid. Shake well to blend; chill. Great on cabbage slaw.

Thousand Island Dressing
Makes about 1½ cups

1 hard-cooked egg, finely chopped
2 teaspoons minced onion
1 cup mayonnaise or salad dressing
¼ cup catsup or chili sauce
2 teaspoons sweet-pickle relish
2 teaspoons minced pimiento-stuffed green olives

Mix all ingredients together and chill about 1 hour. Use to dress hearts of lettuce or tossed green salads.

Russian Dressing
Makes about 1½ cups

1 cup mayonnaise or salad dressing
⅓ cup bottled French dressing
2 tablespoons catsup
2 tablespoons chopped green pepper
1 tablespoon minced onion
½ teaspoon prepared horseradish

Mix all ingredients together and use to dress crisp green salads.

Green Goddess Dressing
Makes about 2½ cups

1 teaspoon leaf tarragon, crumbled
¼ cup tarragon vinegar
1 cup mayonnaise or salad dressing
1 cup dairy sour cream
½ cup chopped fresh parsley
2 tablespoons chopped chives
2 tablespoons anchovy paste
1 tablespoon lemon juice
1 clove garlic, minced

1 Soak tarragon in vinegar 10 minutes; strain vinegar into small mixing bowl; discard tarragon.
2 Blend all remaining ingredients into vinegar; cover and chill 1 to 2 hours. Use to dress crisp green salads.

1662

Tomato French Dressing
Makes 2⅓ cups

Combine 1 cup CLASSIC FRENCH DRESSING with 1 can (10½ ounces) condensed tomato soup, 1 clove garlic, peeled and halved, 1 tablespoon prepared mustard and 1 tablespoon minced onion in a large screw-top jar with a tight-fitting lid. Shake well to blend; chill. Delightful on crisp chilled lettuce wedges.

Blue Cheese French Dressing
Makes 1¼ cups

Combine 1 cup CLASSIC FRENCH DRESSING with ⅓ cup coarsely crumbled blue cheese and 1 clove of garlic, peeled and minced, in a screw-top jar with a tight-fitting lid. Shake well to blend; chill. Zesty on ripe red tomatoes.

INDEX TO RECIPES IN THIS VOLUME

1663

1664